Higher Consciousness

Awakening the Power Within, Expanding Spiritual Awareness, and Elevating Conscious Living

© Copyright 2024 – All rights reserved.

The content contained within this book may not be reproduced, duplicated, or transmitted without direct written permission from the author or the publisher.

Under no circumstances will any blame or legal responsibility be held against the publisher or author for any damages, reparation, or monetary loss due to the information contained within this book, either directly or indirectly.

Legal Notice:

This book is copyright-protected. It is only for personal use. You cannot amend, distribute, sell, use, quote, or paraphrase any part of the content within this book without the consent of the author or publisher.

Disclaimer Notice:

Please note the information contained within this document is for educational and entertainment purposes only. All effort has been executed to present accurate, up-to-date, reliable, and complete information. No warranties of any kind are declared or implied. Readers acknowledge that the author is not engaging in the rendering of legal, financial, medical, or professional advice. The content within this book has been derived from various sources. Please consult a licensed professional before attempting any techniques outlined in this book.

By reading this document, the reader agrees that under no circumstances is the author responsible for any losses, direct or indirect, that are incurred as a result of the use of the information contained within this document, including, but not limited to, errors, omissions, or inaccuracies.

Your Free Gift
(only available for a limited time)

Thanks for getting this book! If you want to learn more about various spirituality topics, then join Mari Silva's community and get a free guided meditation MP3 for awakening your third eye. This guided meditation mp3 is designed to open and strengthen ones third eye so you can experience a higher state of consciousness. Simply visit the link below the image to get started.

https://spiritualityspot.com/meditation

Or, Scan the QR code!

Table of Contents

INTRODUCTION 1
CHAPTER 1: WHAT IS HIGHER CONSCIOUSNESS? 3
CHAPTER 2: THE QUANTUM COSMOS 17
CHAPTER 3: TAP INTO YOUR INNER POWER 29
CHAPTER 4: GO BEYOND TO EXPAND YOUR AWARENESS 40
CHAPTER 5: MEET YOUR HIGHER SELF 51
CHAPTER 6: WORK WITH SPIRIT GUIDES 59
CHAPTER 7: TIMELINES, PAST LIVES, AND SOUL CONTRACTS 67
CHAPTER 8: YOUR HIGHER PURPOSE REVEALED 76
CHAPTER 9: DAILY RITUALS FOR CONSCIOUS LIVING 88
CONCLUSION 96
HERE'S ANOTHER BOOK BY MARI SILVA THAT YOU MIGHT LIKE 98
YOUR FREE GIFT (ONLY AVAILABLE FOR A LIMITED TIME) 99
REFERENCES 100

Introduction

This book will help you to establish a connection to higher consciousness. It is a road map full of valuable information that you will constantly return to as your spiritual life evolves because you'll pick up something new each time you read it.

You may have suspected for the longest time that there is much more to life than meets the eye, and *you're right*. In these pages, you'll find evidence to support your suspicions – and then some.

With this book, you'll blast your eyes wide open (your third eye included) to discover the truth about existence. You'll also wake up the power you carry within you and transform your life into the one you've always dreamed of.

If you're a skeptic about how life works, the groundbreaking discoveries made in the field of quantum physics will be sure to convince you. All your doubts about the creation of reality will be completely cleared up, with everything put into its proper perspective. No longer will you dismiss the law of attraction and other laws of the Universe as mere "woo-woo" talk, especially as you practice what you learn and see the results for yourself.

Unlike other books, this book is written in simple English. You won't be baffled by language or terminology that is difficult to understand. It's one of the most accessible books on consciousness and awakening. Every page is full of powerful, transformational information that will change you, written in a transformational yet comprehensible way.

Loaded with a generous amount of hands-on instructions and methods to help you attain spiritual enlightenment, this is a book that you can't afford to ignore. You'd never deliberately rob yourself of the opportunity of a lifetime, and that's why you'll not only read this book but apply its principles to all you do.

Are you prepared to unlock the doors to wisdom? Do you think you can handle true power? Are you prepared to leave behind everything that has weighed you down and embrace a future full of joy and satisfaction?

All you have to do is walk through the gates to the true reality, leaving behind the world of illusions to find the power that's been waiting within you all this time. So, take a moment to say goodbye to your old self. Your journey to discovering your glorious, Divine Self begins with the first chapter.

Chapter 1: What Is Higher Consciousness?

If you hang around people who dedicate their lives to practicing spirituality long enough, you'll hear the phrase "higher consciousness." But what is it? Is it a being? Is it something ephemeral? Is it somewhere out there over the rainbow or in the depths of your soul? Is it something you need to get or something you *already have?* Is it about being a genius and expressing unparalleled levels of creativity?

What is higher consciousness?
Designed by freepik. https://www.freepik.com/free-vector/gradient-surrealist-galaxy-illustration_45183512.htm

No matter how many questions are swirling around in your mind, your thoughts will be a lot clearer by the end of this book. This first chapter will introduce you to what higher consciousness is. It will show you the different ways to attain this form of consciousness and explain how people connect with it, so the next time you hear your New Age friend or some spiritual teachers say, "higher consciousness," there'll be no doubt in your mind about what they mean.

Consciousness and Its Connection to Quantum Physics

When you're "conscious," you're aware. If you think about it, you're always aware of something. You're aware that you're reading this book. You're aware of the room you're in. You're *conscious* of who you are.

So, a simplistic interpretation of consciousness is the awareness of being. As the late, great Neville Goddard once put it:

"The very center of consciousness is the feeling of I AM. I may forget who I am, where I am, what I am, but I cannot forget that I AM. The awareness of being remains, regardless of the degree of forgetfulness of who, where, and what I am."

For centuries, scientists, psychologists, philosophers, and spiritualists have gone back and forth on what consciousness is. Neville's explanation is one of the easiest to grasp. If you hit your head and lose your memory, forgetting everything you've ever known, you'd at least know you exist.

In this make-believe situation where you've forgotten it all, you'll probably ask, "Who am I? Where am I?" Pay close attention to those questions, and you'll notice you definitely know you are. You experience "I Am" by being aware that you *are*.

Many philosophers over the years have offered their opinions on what consciousness is. The 17th-century philosopher René Descartes once came up with the following theory: Cogito, ergo sum, which means *"I think, therefore I am."* What Descartes's dictum suggests is anyone who's able to think has consciousness.

Ask a psychologist, and they'll tell you that consciousness is a state where you are aware of your surroundings, emotions, thoughts, and feelings. You are about to perceive these things and think about them, as well. This is your subjective experience of life as you observe it in your outer and inner worlds.

Sigmund Freud, the psychologist who created and developed psychoanalysis, believed the mind comprises three distinct parts: the conscious, the preconscious, and the unconscious. According to Freud, your conscious mind is everything you are aware of. Your preconscious mind is the part of you with emotions and thoughts that can become conscious when you pause and reflect. Finally, there's your unconscious mind, which contains all the memories and desires you can't consciously think of or access.

Ask a scientist what consciousness is, and they'll tell you it's a product of the brain. From a scientific perspective, it's impossible to be conscious or aware without a living, functioning brain that has every neuron doing its job. Francis Crick and Christof Koch are two brilliant neuroscientists who claim the neural networks in that amazing organ in your skull are responsible for giving you the ability to know you exist in the world around you – and to process your inner experiences as well. Yet, scientists haven't cracked the code of the neurobiological mechanisms that lead to consciousness. It's still a mystery – at least, according to scientists who don't subscribe to quantum ideas or the paranormal.

Now, what about quantum physics, also called *quantum mechanics*? This form of physics is focused on understanding phenomena you can only observe on the smallest of scales. It's all about how molecules, atoms, and subatomic particles work and interact. Look at life through the quantum lens, and you'll find all sorts of strange things that don't line up with regular classical physics!

According to classical physics, when you throw a ball up in the air, it must land, right? You've likely seen this happen countless times. In quantum physics, the ball might disappear, then pop back into existence, change colors at a speed faster than light, and then land – *probably*. That's because there are more possibilities besides the ball simply landing.

What's the connection between consciousness and quantum mechanics? Experts in this field claim consciousness is the result of activity that takes place on the quantum level. Multiple theories on the quantum mechanical production of consciousness exist, collectively called Quantum Mind Theories. You didn't pick this book up to learn the ins and outs of quantum mechanics in detail, but it helps to know some of the major points in this field that are connected to consciousness.

Wave Function Collapse: In quantum physics, the universe is an ocean full of endless possibilities that are all happening simultaneously. This concept is the *wave function*. In the world as you know it, when you toss a coin, it's either going to be heads or tails. In the quantum world, it's both heads and tails at the same time. This state is called superposition, but the moment you look at the coin, you cause a wave function collapse, forcing it to be either heads or tails.

This suggests your consciousness or mind is the cause of the wave function collapse. Your observation, part of your consciousness, causes you to experience life as you do. If you'd like to experience something else, you have to turn your attention away from the current reality to a different one out of the endless possibilities available.

Quantum Brain Mechanics: Think of each brain cell as part of an orchestra. Each neuron has a different role to play, but it works along with all the others to create a beautiful piece of music, which is, in this context, your consciousness. Physicists understand that this symphony is the result of quantum processes.

Experts suggest that the microtubules in the brain cells cause consciousness. The microtubules of the neurons are in a superposition, similar to the coin that's both heads and. This is the concept of quantum brain dynamics.

Entanglement: Pretend you're holding two dice in one hand. When you roll them, each one will stop on whatever number it does, and neither is controlled or influenced by the other. Yet, in quantum physics, these dice are entangled, which means no matter how far apart they are from each other, the result you get after rolling one will immediately affect another. This strange quantum magic is called entanglement. This isn't a mere theory. It's already been observed and confirmed by these brilliant quantum scientists.

The connection between the concept of entanglement and consciousness should be obvious. Whatever you are conscious of – whatever your thoughts and emotions are – is reflected in your reality. Wake up thinking it's going to be a bad day, and watch how hard life works to give you things to complain about. Entanglement suggests that your consciousness has a deep connection with reality as you experience it.

Higher Consciousness

If consciousness is seeing a tree, higher consciousness is seeing the tree, the entire forest, and then some. It is awareness on steroids. It's perceiving things beyond your ordinary consciousness's capacity to pick up. This form of consciousness isn't just about knowing where you are, who you are, and how you feel. It transcends your subjective experience of life and connects with something more significant, or, as some would put it, the divine or universal consciousness.

When you connect with higher consciousness, you are connected to a state of awareness that is beyond yourself. It's a state beyond your limited ego, which is why it's also called expanded consciousness. Some think of it as a part of the brain that people have access to now and then, and not for long each time. You could consider it the opposite of your primal desires and instincts.

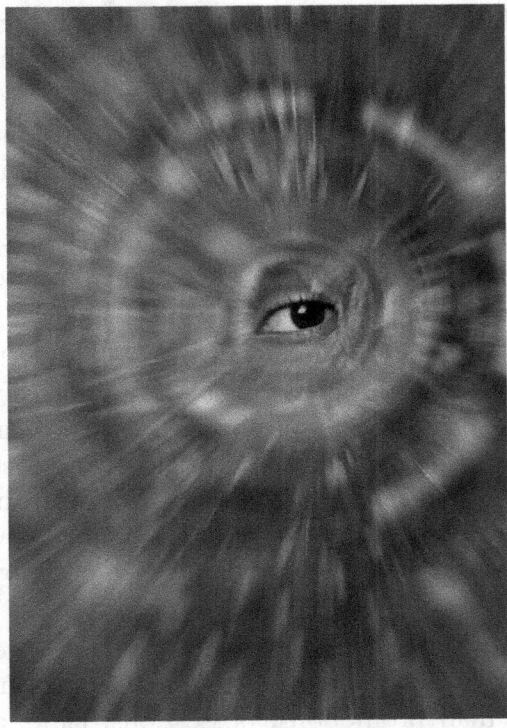

Higher consciousness is perceiving things beyond your ordinary consciousness's capacity to pick up.
Designed by freepik. https://www.freepik.com/free-photo/br_own-eye-bright-background_31499094.htm

Most people live their lives in lower consciousness, which is also known as the ego. The ego isn't a bad thing because it has its function. After all, there's no way to live in this modern world without it, but the trick lies in knowing that it's not you. It's a costume, and like all costumes, it can be changed. Identifying as your ego means you shut yourself out of the world of possibilities available to you.

Your ego is the sum of everything you think you are, your assumptions about yourself and others. The most self-involved people function from the ego alone. When you tap into higher consciousness, you're less selfish and more self-aware. Your heart is full of compassion and empathy, and it feels natural to be kind. Every decision you make using higher consciousness is rooted in love rather than fear.

Why does higher consciousness matter? What use is it to you? If your spiritual development is important to you, then it would serve you to learn more about higher consciousness and how to tap into it every day. On the surface, it seems like there's nothing more important than having a job, paying your rent, staying up to date with the news and new technology, etc.

Achieving success, having a high status in society, and increasing the number of zeros in your bank account seem so crucial in today's world, but most people are missing one truth. Success in all its forms can only come to you if you're willing to develop yourself. True self-development begins from within. It starts with you becoming aware of your spiritual self.

Fulfillment comes from feeding your soul with everything it needs to express itself more fully through your life every day. Everything in the physical world is the result of spiritual action. You can't take enough physical action to get the feeling of satisfaction that every human instinctively desires and reaches for – unless you learn how to live from the perspective of higher consciousness. Doing this, you are *"tuned in, tapped in, and turned on,"* as Abraham, channeled by Esther Hicks, says.

If you find yourself feeling dissatisfied with life lately, it could be because you are finally waking up to the fact that there are more important things than promotions, possessions, fame, and status. You could be at the top of the pyramid, rubbing shoulders with the crème de la crème, and still feel empty if your soul is starving for a connection to divinity.

Some think that once they reach higher consciousness, nothing bad will ever happen, and there will be smooth seas and clear skies in the scheme of things from that point on. You start receiving inspirational ideas that lead you to where you need to go when you act on them. Your perception of yourself is clearer as you become more aware of yourself and the reality of life.

This increase in awareness is never-ending. There is no final destination where you "retire" from spiritual work and enjoy the benefits indefinitely. There's an ebb and flow, times where you're more tapped in than others.

It's like being a professional soccer player. You know how to pass, shoot, and dribble. No denying that you're good on the field, but that doesn't mean you never make mistakes. Sometimes, you make a pass, but an opponent intercepts the ball. Sometimes, you try a sliding tackle, but you miss and wind up with a yellow card.

In the same way, there will be times you forget to stay connected to your higher consciousness. When this happens, you regress to being who you were before you began your conscious spiritual journey, living from the mindsets of fear and limitation. You don't have to be afraid of this, though, because when you fall, you can always get back up and keep going.

Methods of Attaining Higher Consciousness

Humanity has used various methods to attain higher consciousness for hundreds of years. Monks, shamans, and yogis are some of those who have always known how to set their egos aside and connect with the infinite intelligence of the higher mind.

Fortunately, you won't have to sequester yourself away in some monastery or remote region to tap into the spiritual reality of life. The methods used to get to this state of awareness are accessible to you here and now. Here is a quick look at some of them.

Meditation and Mindfulness: Meditation is deliberately focusing your attention on one thing. Your point of focus could be an object like a candle's flame or a spot on the wall. You may prefer to focus on your breathing or count a specific sequence of numbers. You can keep your attention on a mantra, a short word or phrase that carries a spiritual energy you'll experience the more you focus on it. By focusing on one thing only, you become a master at directing your attention. With practice, you'll be calmer and more stable, regardless of what you're experiencing in life.

Another form of meditation is mindfulness. This practice is about becoming conscious of yourself and every moment. You learn to be aware of what your mind is up to by noticing your thoughts without judgment. You pay attention to what you experience on the inside and the outside through your five senses. You notice every desire and feeling that arises within you, neither judging nor identifying with it. If you're always anxious about your future or regretful about your past, you'll find mindfulness a useful practice because it grounds you in the present.

Contemplation: When you take time to think deeply and reflect on something, you are contemplating it. Think of it as a form of meditation, except this time, you're focusing on an idea, a question, or even a verse from a sacred, spiritual text. There are no limits to the subjects you can contemplate. You could reflect deeply on the nature of reality, what the solution to a problem would look like, your life's purpose, the person you have been versus who you'd like to become, etc.

Contemplation is not the same thing as thinking in the usual sense. It has nothing to do with planning your day or being concerned about what tomorrow will be like. All you do when you contemplate is allow your mind to settle on that question or idea you want to focus on. You trust that whatever you need to know as you contemplate this thing will blossom in your mind. It's not about trying to figure it out on your own. Instead, you're keeping your mind open and giving yourself space to allow information related to the subject you're contemplating to come up within you.

Fasting: Before anything else, if you decide to take the fasting route to higher consciousness, please check with your medical health professional first to ensure there is nothing to be worried about. You know what they say – *better safe than sorry.*

Fasting is a spiritual practice that has existed for thousands of years and is still practiced worldwide today. Most people in Western society are quick to condemn anyone who practices fasting. Part of that reasoning is the result of capitalism, which has sold people ideas like "breakfast is the most important meal of the day" – just so a certain company can sell as many cereal boxes as possible!

When you fast, you abstain from food for a fixed period. You could also abstain from drinking anything (that would be a *dry fast*). A fast can be as short as a few hours or as long as weeks. By fasting, you purify your body and mind. In this pure state, it's easier to tap into higher consciousness and gain perspectives you'd never have if you were feasting as usual.

This practice helps you discipline your body and mind, reminding you that you are in control of these things and not the other way around. The clarity and inner peace you get from a fast help you remove spiritual or energetic blocks to experiencing higher consciousness in your life. Fasting brings you in touch with the subtle parts of yourself that you don't often think about.

Chanting and Mantras: When you chant, you repeat a specific word or phrase, and this brings you into the higher consciousness state. Chanting is an ancient spiritual practice, and the fact that people still do it today is a testament to how effective it is for tapping into higher consciousness. You could either chant aloud or silently in your mind. It's similar to meditation, except your point of focus is whatever you're chanting.

Mantras are sounds, words, or phrases you repeat as you meditate. You may assume it's the same thing as chanting, but there's a slight difference. Chanting is broader, as it's speaking or singing repetitively. You could chant a word, melody, or tone.

On the other hand, a mantra is a specific kind of chant. It is used in Buddhism, Hinduism, and a few other traditions. These mantras are usually short and have a profound spiritual effect on you when you use them. All mantras are chanted, but not every chant is a mantra. Regardless of what you choose, these tools will give you the divine connection you seek.

Yoga: Many assume yoga is only about physical poses and keeping fit. This practice has existed for thousands of years, originating in ancient India. Other than poses, yoga involves breathing techniques and meditation practices. Yoga is from the Sanskrit word yuj, meaning "to unite or yoke." This spiritual practice aims to achieve unity between your awareness and higher consciousness.

In yoga, the physical postures are called asanas. By practicing these postures, you prepare your body for meditation. As you flow from one posture to another, you quiet your mind. You become present, which is the best state for effective meditation.

By practicing these postures, you prepare your body for meditation.
https://www.pexels.com/photo/woman-in-pink-sports-bra-and-black-leggings-doing-yoga-on-yoga-mat-3823076/

The breathing techniques are called pranayama. Yogis have always believed that the connection between your body and mind is in the breath – and they're not wrong. The next time you're in a fit of anger, slow your breath down. Make it long and deep, and notice how your mind relaxes.

Once you control your breath, you control your mind and the flow of energy in your body. When your body and mind are in the perfect state to connect with the spirit world, you can use any of the yoga techniques, including mantra meditation, concentration, and mindfulness. This is another path to higher consciousness.

Entheogens: In shamanic traditions, people – usually shamans – use entheogens to connect with higher consciousness. The word "entheogen" is from Greek, and it means "generating the divine within" or "generating God within." Also called sacraments, these are substances that induce an altered state of consciousness, allowing the shamans or the people they lead to connect to higher states of consciousness.

To be clear, this book is not encouraging or endorsing drug abuse. If this is an experience you'd like to have, it's best to go with a professional and get confirmation from your doctor that it's safe for you.

The cultures and traditions that use entheogens do not do so for fun. These tools are holy and sacred to them because they allow people to directly experience divinity. These substances rip off the veil of physical reality, allowing you to experience true reality, which is oneness, love, and light.

There are various kinds of entheogens, from synthesized versions like LSD to natural ones like psilocybin mushrooms and peyote. The peyote cactus has been used for spiritual purposes for more than 2,000 years in Mesoamerica. It's still popular among the Huichol Indians of Mexico. These sacraments give you insight and a broader view of life than anything you could imagine.

You're right to suspect there's some controversy around the use of sacraments, as some are concerned about the risks to physical and mental health when used in any other context than traditionally or with the help of experienced guides. For this reason, many of these substances are regulated or outlawed in most places. Regardless of the fearmongering, entheogens are undeniable gateways to higher consciousness.

Ethical living: When you choose to live according to ethics and principles like nonviolence, truthfulness, generosity, kindness, etc., you achieve the purity of mind that makes it easier to attain higher consciousness. You have a moral code and decide never to act outside of it.

It makes no sense to meditate every day, first thing in the morning, only to harm others by being dishonest and cruel or deliberately triggering people. There's a reason many spiritual traditions encourage living ethically in addition to other practices for connecting with divinity.

Living by ethics requires self-awareness. Self-awareness makes you more conscious of other aspects of yourself connected with the Higher Mind. It's not just that you don't hurt people, but you also take every chance you get to cultivate positivity. You care about other people's well-being and yours. This is why Buddhism proposes the Five Moral Precepts:
- Respect for life
- Generosity
- Responsible relationships
- Truthful communication

- Mindfulness

When you live according to these ethics, you keep your mind pure and reduce the noise that drowns out the voice of spirit within you. Your awareness expands, helping you attain higher consciousness. If you're about to take action and unsure if you've made the right decision, think about whether that choice aligns with your spiritual goals, and you'll have your answer.

How Higher Consciousness Changes Your Life

"I experience peace every day – even when I shouldn't."

"I used to be the most anxious person I knew. I can't believe once upon a time, I thought that was something to be proud of. I thought it meant I thought of everything so I'd never be caught off guard. Over the years, that anxiety became such a burden that I couldn't function. Panic attacks became the norm for me. I had a nagging feeling that I needed to take up meditation, but I had no idea how to do it in the first place. After doing my homework, I began to meditate every day for 10 minutes.

"The effects of my daily meditation practice began subtly at first. Something happened at work, and one of my coworkers pointed out that they were surprised I didn't panic as usual. After that day, I began paying closer attention to myself. I noticed the space between my triggers and the reactions that followed. In the past, I would have reacted without thinking. Now, thanks to my connection with higher consciousness, I'm more aware of my emotions. I can feel them without letting them steal my peace – no matter if I'm having a good day or a bad one." - Jane

~~~~~~

"I fell in love with myself."

"For a long time, I never liked myself. That's putting it mildly because I loathed who I was. I did a good job covering that up by acting confident, sometimes to the point of arrogance. But I was filled with shame and guilt for years. I thought that was life and everyone felt the same. It was only after a conversation with a trusted friend that I realized I had a problem. As heavy as the burden I carried was, it was good to know that there were other ways to be besides how I'd been living.

I started going to therapy, where I discovered the past trauma I'd gone through and what limiting beliefs I had that affected every part of my life since I was a child. I realized the person that I'd been all this time wasn't really who I was. I was a living trauma response. When I started doing spiritual practices alongside my therapy, this was when my healing reached new levels. One of the most profound experiences for me was connecting with higher consciousness through meditation and contemplation. I had an amazing session where I was suddenly overwhelmed with a feeling that I didn't have a word for. If there's a word for 'the greatest love ever,' that would be it because four letters don't describe what I felt that day.

"I felt reborn. I felt awake for the first time in my life. I felt this greatest love flowing through my body, overwhelming my mind to the point of its nonexistence and bursting out of my being. If I had anticipated this, I'd have taken a moment to mourn my former self. The old Jared that got me to that point had died that day.

"Later, I learned that this was the "ego death" experience. It was more than the realization that I didn't have to be the person I'd always been. More than that, I couldn't relate to my old self anymore. I now understand that I have one purpose in life, and that is to love everything, everyone, and, just as importantly, myself. Not for anything I stand to gain, but just because." - Jared

These are just two stories about how your connection with higher consciousness can radically transform your life for the better. Here are more ways that your connection with Divinity will affect you:

1. Your energy becomes softer as you release anger, aggression, and pain. This leads you to have a better attitude about your life.
2. You'll be more in touch with your intuition and learn to follow it without question.
3. You'll drop bad habits and pick up new, better ones. You may have new hobbies or interests and meet new people who line up with your energy. You may even switch careers, preferring something simpler and less demanding.
4. You'll reduce your materialism. This happens because you recognize there are more important things in life than money and stuff.
5. You accept responsibility for your life, knowing that you are where you are because of you and nothing else. You no longer play the blame game - even with yourself. Holding

yourself accountable doesn't mean bashing yourself for past bad decisions. It's knowing if you got yourself into something, you could get yourself out of it. It's taking action.

6. You no longer expect people and things to make you happy because as you attain higher consciousness, you recognize that happiness is an inside job. You also stop defining yourself as a success or a failure based on what the world says or your old limiting beliefs.

7. You experience more miracles and synchronistic events. Everything about life is synchronicity, but when you attain higher consciousness, this synchronicity becomes clear as day. You recognize that you are in a never-ending dance with infinite intelligence. You've always been, but you didn't realize it until you woke up.

Higher consciousness allows you to do so much for yourself and others. Do you feel lost and confused? Would you like the most reliable guidance about how to handle a situation? Is there a problem you've been trying to solve that's proven difficult to crack? Do you need physical, emotional, or mental healing? No matter what you need help with, you will get your answers once you connect with a higher consciousness.

You'll know that you've attained this altered state of being when you experience it. There will be no doubt in your mind. This is the same state that shamans enter to work in the spiritual world. Higher consciousness is the origin of intuition, which is inner teaching and knowing that is beyond whatever your rational mind can come up with. You can experience this in lucid dreams, where you are awake and conscious within your dream, exploring the worlds within. This is the same as Christ-consciousness and God-consciousness, a state full of wisdom, love, and understanding. It is the Buddhist Nirvana where you are set free from the illusions of this physical world.

The vastness of the universe is beyond comprehension. It continues to expand outward and inward into infinity. You are an intricate part of the universe. There is no disconnection between you. You are entangled, as the quantum physicists say. So, if you want to know more about yourself, you should learn as much as you can about the universe. Where do you begin? Find out in the next chapter.

Chapter 2: The Quantum Cosmos

"As above, so below. As within, so without. As the Universe, so the soul." – Hermes Trismegistus, The Kybalion

Now that you have a solid understanding of what higher consciousness means and you're familiar with the bit of quantum mechanics, it's time to take a look at the universe itself. There's so much to ponder about the universe. How exactly did it come into existence? If The Big Bang led to the creation of the universe, then what caused The Big Bang? If something or someone caused The Big Bang, who or where are they? They have to be somewhere, which would mean there is more than one universe, right? Did their universe begin with a Big Bang too? If it did, what or who caused their version of the Big Bang? Just how many Big Bangs ar there? Is the entirety of existence done Big-Banging around, or still at it?

If The Big Bang led to the creation of the universe, then what caused The Big Bang?
Designed by freepik. https://www.freepik.com/free-photo/ultra-detailed-nebula-abstract-wallpaper-5_39994515.htm

There are still more questions to consider. If the world is still expanding, what is the point of it all? What part are you supposed to play in this vast cosmos? You may think that God has all the answers, but that raises a new set of questions. Who is God? Where is God? Who or what is the source of existence itself? What's the deal with all the deities across cultures, traditions, and religions?

Turn your attention to outer space, and you'll find even more questions burning within you. If time passes differently within a black hole, what is the true nature of time? Is it real? What makes reality real?

If you're going to ask questions about time, you may also question its counterpart, space. What is space? Is it real? What does it mean if you are a fractal of the universe? If every part of the universe is reflected in your being, does that mean you're a universe? Would that imply that all space between things doesn't exist? If you're a universe, are there Big Bangs happening inside of the inside of your inside, ad nauseam?

This chapter will help you understand everything about your place in the universe. You'll develop an expanded awareness of life. It's essential to finish this chapter before moving on to the next because it's the key to unlocking a deeper understanding of the subjects discussed in the chapters to come.

The Birth of the Universe

Where did the universe come from? Many theories seek to answer this question, but one of the most accepted ones all over the world is The Big Bang theory. This theory says the universe began from one atom that existed before time itself and then rapidly expanded in a cataclysm of cosmic proportions. According to Big Bang theorists, the universe started from a compact size. How compact, you wonder? The answer is about a million billion billionth of the size of one atom.

The energy of this primordial atom was denser than anything imaginable. Its density was so great that it combined electromagnetism, gravity, and the strong and weak nuclear forces, creating a single one. Over time, as matter cooled down from the bang, more particles formed. More time passed, and these particles became the stars and galaxies you know.

You can't talk about the universe without discussing dark matter and energy. These two things are still mysterious, but there's no doubt they are responsible for the creation of the cosmos. Dark matter is a different kind of matter. It never interacts with light, which means there's no way to see it. The only reason you know it exists is because of the gravitational effects it has on galaxies and galaxy clusters. It's like Gorilla glue on a cosmic level, as this dark matter keeps all the galaxies together where they need to be.

The Big Bang left behind a soup of particles that continue to expand and cool down, all thanks to dark matter.

On the other hand, you have *dark energy*. This particular kind of energy is in all space and is why the universe continues expanding faster. The intriguing thing about dark energy and dark matter is they are 95% of the universe. The remaining 5% is all the regular matter that you see every day. That should make you wonder what's going on with the 95%.

At least five billion years ago, the rate of acceleration of the universe's expansion picked up speed. After much research, scientists have concluded that it must be dark energy causing this acceleration. While they're still at a loss as to the true nature of dark energy, the effects of this energy are undeniable. It's a force that increases the space between galaxies, which leads to the ultimate expansion of the universe.

There's a delicate balance between dark matter and dark energy. Dark matter helps to keep things together through gravity, while dark energy pushes things apart, which causes the expansion of the universe. You could say these two phenomena are the architects of the history and the future of the universe. Scientists believe the more they understand these mysterious twin forces, the better they can tell where the universe is going and how to prepare for that destination.

Multiple Universes?

The multiverse theory suggests that there are many other universes besides this one. This is something phenomenal to ponder because the universe you're in is already vast. It's full of hundreds of billions of galaxies. How many stars are in your universe? They are beyond counting. It's even more mind-boggling to realize that the stars and galaxies exist throughout 10s of billions of light years. In other words, take 9.4607, multiply that by 10 to the power of 12, and you get almost 6,000,000 million miles.

Now multiply that figure by 10s of billions, and it's immediately evident that one universe alone is a lot. So, the thought that there may be other universes besides this one is both amazing and terrifying. There might be many versions of you out there doing exactly what you're doing, and many more being versions of yourself that you could never imagine, doing things that have never crossed your mind.

The multiverse theory also suggests that each of these universes could have entirely different laws of physics by which they operate. There could also be other life forms that you aren't familiar with. As your body is a universe of individual cells, life could be a collection of universes – a multiverse. This is a theory that is debated in philosophy and physics.

One of the most prominent depictions of the multiverse is rooted in inflation theory. According to this theory, an event occurred when the universe was in its infancy – the briefest period since it came into existence. This infinitesimally short amount of time was when the universe began its rapid expansion, or inflation, to become incomprehensibly larger than its size before the inflation.

Experts claim the universe you're in stopped its inflation 14 billion years ago, but the fascinating thing is, just because the inflation has ended with this universe does not mean it's ended everywhere else. So, right now, multiple universes are still experiencing inflation. This universe is simply one of many universes that pinch from much larger ones still in the expansion process. The process is eternal, creating more and more singular universes.

The theory that life is eternally inflating means each universe should have its laws and particles. Each one has forces that it respects. The constants of each universe are also different from here on Earth, and that's why it's nearly impossible to explain dark matter with regular classical physics.

Is there any validity in the idea that there is a multiverse? If you think about it, it's the fact that there is life at all. This universe has been specially orchestrated to allow intelligent life forms to exist that can observe the cosmos. It seems as though some intelligent force has set things up deliberately to support life.

Think about how abundant carbon is. Consider the importance of light for photosynthesis, which allows plants to grow and sustain all other living beings. How convenient is it that a big ball of light is up in the sky, helping plants grow and thrive? All of these things together couldn't possibly be a coincidence. The existence of life, as you know it, suggests an intelligence responsible for creating it.

Certain versions of the multiverse theory suggest every decision you make causes a new universe to be created. This is where you have the concept of parallel realities. Are you starting to realize how expansive and intricate all of life is?

Your Soul's Role in the Vast Cosmos

If all of life continues to expand and there are many versions of you, the question to ask is, what is your purpose in life? What role is your soul supposed to play in this cosmos? It may almost appear that all of it is meaningless if you attempt to answer those questions through the lens of the limited human paradigm, which assumes things gain more value if they are scarce and vice versa. That's certainly one way to think about it.

Think about the fact that the whole is the sum of its parts. You are part of the universe, which means you have a part to play. You are inherently relevant and of great value. Without you, the world would not be as it is. Your perspective and ability to observe the world is an intricate part of the existence of life. The finite and infinite may seem separate, but they are one.

Imagine you're a drop of the ocean. At first, you may assume that you are irrelevant compared to this huge body of water. From your limited perspective, it's clear why you'd think this way. Now imagine every other drop in the ocean thinks the same way that you do. Each one decides to go its own way. What would be left of the ocean? Nothing.

You are performing your soul's sole purpose by being yourself.
Designed by freepik. Source: https://www.freepik.com/free-vector/hand-drawn-mindfulness-concept-with-characters_16692663.htm

Your soul has its part to play. This truth echoes across various cultures, traditions, and faiths, demonstrating how essential you are to life. The light of creation shines through your unique state of being, experiences, and interpretations of said experiences. You express the power of divinity, whether you see it as the omniscient Abrahamic God, the impersonal Hinduist Brahman, or that which connects one and all as in Taoism. Whatever labels you use to express this divine essence, the point is that it exists, and simply by being yourself here and now, you are performing your soul's sole purpose: to reflect and express the Source of all life.

The idea of multiple universes may not exist in every spiritual tradition, but reincarnation is an interesting parallel. Reincarnation is when a single consciousness or soul explores different lives in the same universe. Since the multiverse theory suggests there's more than one universe, your soul can experience itself within more than one reality, facing unique challenges and different goals in each one. You are a part of the whole, doing your part for the evolution of consciousness.

This idea is synonymous with the beliefs held in tradition, similar to Sufism. You contain the perfection of the divine source of all things, and your life itself is the process of revealing this perfection. It's the same idea as the Buddha nature, where the goal is to become enlightened, or in the Hindu understanding of the True Self, also called the Atman. Before creation, all things were one thing. For this one thing to know itself fully, it had to create another. As a result, the one thing has become what it is and what it is not – which is also part of what it is.

In simple English, you are the Source of all life, understanding itself through your perspective and experience of itself as "not-Source." How do you know what cold water is if you've never touched hot water? How do you know North if there is no South? How do you know who you are without also knowing who you aren't? Therefore, your soul's ultimate purpose is the grand revelation of the Creator.

If you've always wondered where God, deities, and other beings fit into the ever-expanding puzzle of existence, the answer must have become apparent to you by now. There are many names to describe this one force that created and still creates all things. Many stories attempt to capture the essence of this same thing, which is less a thing and more like a being that embodies infinite intelligence and all of existence. Regardless of religion or tradition, they all attempt to capture the same thing: the story of the Creator of the universe, still in the process of creating.

As there is an omniscient God, there are other beings that are emanations of God, "less than" the Creator in the sense that they, too, have been created. In the Kabbalah, they're called the Sefirot, emanations of Ein Sof, the infinite Unknowable God. These emanations are the different aspects of divinity responsible for guiding humanity to ultimate enlightenment.

Think of these as the angels, guides, and other beings who are said to guide humanity's spiritual evolution and help them navigate the maze of life on Earth with increasing grace and wisdom. Whatever name you assign it, there's a single Source from which all deities and other lesser divine beings spring.

Across spiritual traditions, you'll find guides, teachers, and deities playing critical roles that all assist the human soul on its journey to enlightenment, which is unity with the Source of all life. These beings have enough experience, having traveled much further along their evolution. From their evolved state, they reach out to the travelers coming behind them. They're here to say to you, as in the book of Isaiah, chapter 30, verse 21, "...*This is the way, walk ye in it...*"

Deities, guides, ascended masters, angels, and other similar entities share the knowledge they gleaned from when they were where humanity is presently in their respective journeys. These beings benevolently guide everyone back home to their true self. They have embodied higher consciousness in ways that humanity is yet to achieve, so their guidance is a helpful gift.

As for the Source they (and you) come from, it lacks personality – not because it's boring, but because it contains all personalities itself by being the space and power behind the creation and evolution of galaxies and the life forms each one carries. Whether it's the idea of a creator or deities and other beings, you must wonder about the observer effect and its implications.

According to this quantum physics tenet, by observing something, you affect the way it behaves. This begs the question, is humanity in some way influencing the existence of these deities and beings? Are people simply interpreting formless energy and consciousness through the lens of these traditional and spiritual beliefs, creating real experiences of these beings and their abilities?

Are the people who meet and connect with these beings, whether in real life, dreams, or visions, simply summoning them through the power of their belief? Also, when you have more than enough people believing in the same thing, surely that should be enough to create an entire universe of spiritual beings, shouldn't it? If the observer effect is true – and it is – does that imply you, too, are a creator? There are no right or wrong answers per se. These questions are simply interesting to ponder.

If you've studied spiritualism, you know there must be a spirit world. This world exists beyond the physical. It's a world where things you'd consider impossible are possible. In this space, you'd expect to see ancestral spirits, guides, and other beings you may not ever have read, heard, or thought about. People connect with these beings either on their own or with the assistance of genuine psychics and mediums. You, too, have received messages from the spiritual world if you've noticed synchronicity, those meaningful coincidences that force you to pause and be here, now.

With this fresh perspective, your interaction and connection with your God or other deity should evolve. You now understand that you weren't meant to accomplish your soul's mission in a bubble. There is an entire team that would be happy to assist you, at least according to spiritualism and religious beliefs. Even if you consider yourself an atheist, it's nice to know that there is an infinite neutral force you can rally to your goals. Whether you call it willpower, focus, determination, or attention, it's all one and the same energy. It's a higher consciousness.

Time, Reality, Fractals

When you think about time, chances are you consider it linear. You think of the past, the present, and the future. Quantum physics doesn't view time in that way. Instead, time is interconnected. The past, present, and future do not flow sequentially.

If you close your eyes and try to replicate the events of yesterday at 4:00 PM, you would be in that time right now. If you imagine a possible future for tomorrow at 5:00 PM, you would be in one of many parallel realities where that is exactly what took place right now. Everything is here and now. There is neither before nor after. You only perceive it that way because of the physics of this world. On a quantum level, it's all happening right now.

Even spiritual traditions have interesting things to say about this. Your past, present, and future all exist, whether you perceive them right now or not. This idea of time is the principle behind such manifestation methods, such as using your imagination to go back in time and change what happened so it lines up with the present or future you'd rather experience.

What makes reality real? From everything you now know, you can infer that there is an ultimate reality. You can also infer that there are subjective forms of reality. There are as many realities as there are people. Even if there's someone in the room with you right now, you are both experiencing two completely different versions of reality.

This becomes even more complex when you consider what's happening in your inner world versus theirs. While you may be sitting in front of a laptop trying to figure out the next words to write in a chapter of your great novel, they may be on vacation somewhere in the Cayman Islands, sipping on a Mai Tai in their imagination.

Some suggest that any reality that cannot be observed by people other than yourself is not real. That's a rather reductive way to think of reality. If you wanted to go along with their argument, what would they say about people who experience shared visions and dreams? Some have a more generous definition of reality, claiming that if you cannot perceive it, it isn't real. This definition does away with the need for other observers in the room.

However, if this were true, what about all those times you were stuck in an anxiety dream, for instance? When you're in the middle of dreaming, the world around you feels real, but when you awaken, you no longer have access to that world. You cannot perceive it unless you go back to bed and pick up where you left off in that dream.

So, according to the proponents of the second definition of reality, your dream world went from being real to unreal, and that's not logical.

The truth is there are many layers to reality. There's the physical world you pick up on with your five senses, but that's only one of many realms. The physical world is the product of a much deeper reality made of pure consciousness. It is the source of all things and beings, as well as events that have happened, are happening, and will happen. This resonates with the spiritual concept of the Akashic records, a spiritual storehouse of all experiences and kinds of knowledge in existences known and unknown.

Things get even more interesting when you consider the quantum physics side of things, where the observer effect suggests that reality is pliable. If you can mold it to fit your preferences and expectations, in much the same way you control what happens in a lucid dream, the question becomes this: *Are you awake, are you dreaming, or is it all the same thing so it doesn't matter anyway?*

It is said that every person is a fractal of the universe. A fractal is a pattern that repeats itself in the whole of a thing as well as its parts. Think of the Fibonacci sequence, for instance, which shows up in all sorts of objects, from flowers to buildings. Your soul is a fractal of the source of all things.

The fact that everything in life is fractal is what makes it possible for you to find analogies in nature to explain your life experiences. It is why if you strip different systems down to their core, whether religious, financial, political, industrial, or otherwise, you can find similar patterns repeating themselves in terms of how these systems run and how those who operate within them behave.

This sentiment of being a fractal of the universe demonstrates that there is no separation between you and everything else in life. The web of divinity connects one and all, whether you are conscious of it or not. This is not to say there is no relevance to your unique individual perspectives and experiences, but that you are part of a grander whole.

This chapter has one purpose: to blast your mind wide open regarding these concepts and have only one perspective of time, the one you perceive. As a result, it is nearly impossible to access higher consciousness and change your life radically. You've been taught that reality is fixed and relentlessly continues as it is through time unless and until someone with great vision changes things. With this chapter, you now know what Louise Hay meant by her quote, *"The point of power is in the present."* You don't have to settle for things when you can make them as you prefer.

You've also been taught to view yourself as separate from everyone else. Once you question this idea you've been spoon-fed all your life, you'll realize that part of the blocks you experience in your attempts to create the life you prefer is this idea of being apart from everything and everyone else. This belief is a wall that keeps you from what you should receive.

Think of it like this. If you are yourself and the person who has something you need, why would you not give yourself what you seek? You already have it. Knowing you're one and the same as others who seem different is one of the keys to receiving your desires in the physical world. The moment you become conscious of the truth that you are everyone, and as Neville Goddard put it, *"everyone is you pushed out,"* you will experience miracles like never before.

Visualization Exercise – Connecting with the Universe's Energy

Don't be intimidated by the word "visualization." It's the same as imagination. The following is an exercise to help you get in touch with the feeling of connection between yourself and the universe. You'll get the most out of this visualization exercise if you do it somewhere free from distractions.

If you live with other people, please ask them to give you at least 10 to 15 minutes with no disturbance. If you have any devices with you, it's best to leave them outside the space or turn them off so you're not distracted by notifications, alarms, or phone calls. Ensure you're wearing comfortable clothing that allows you to breathe and move freely, and check the room's temperature so it's not uncomfortably hot or cold.

1. Sit or lie down in a comfortable position. Close your eyes.
2. Pay attention to your breathing. Notice the inhales and exhales. With time, each will naturally become deeper and longer. When you feel a sense of presence or stillness within you, you're ready for the next step.
3. Pretend you're floating gently off whatever you're resting on. Feel what it would be like to have gravity release you as you float higher and higher.
4. Imagine floating up through your roof and into the sky. Watch the clouds pass you by as you head higher and higher.
5. Now you're in space, a dark backdrop with many twinkling stars as far as your imaginary eyes can see. Feel the sense of wonder fill your heart and soul as you realize you're looking at the universe.
6. Now, look down at your whole body, from your chest to your feet. Notice your body emitting a soft glow that gradually

shines brighter. Feel your body, heart, and soul becoming one with this light. Know that you, too, are now a star.

7. In your star form, imagine you can see glowing threads of energy in the form of light, connecting you to all the stars and planets around you, as well as every life form in the universe.

8. Notice energy flowing back and forth between you and everything else. You're connected to it all.

9. Feel your ego dissolve as you lose your sense of self and become one with everything. Feel the power, peace, connection, and wholeness permeating all of you to the point where you become the whole.

10. Remain in this state for as long as you desire or until your timer alerts you.

11. When you're ready to return, take a few conscious, gentle breaths. Give your toes and fingers a wiggle to become aware of your body once more. Then, after counting down slowly from five to one, open your eyes.

You've just felt the raw power of the connection you have with the Universe or, if you prefer, with the Source of life. Do this exercise each day, and watch how radically your mind and life are transformed for the better.

Now you know about the true nature of reality and time, how the universe came to be, what your soul's mission is, and what God and the other divine beings have to do with it all, it's time to learn about the vast treasure house you carry within you in the next chapter.

Chapter 3: Tap into Your Inner Power

"Knowing others is intelligence; knowing yourself is true wisdom. Mastering others is strength; mastering yourself is true power." - Lao Tzu, Tao Te Ching

For a long time, humanity has been preoccupied with discovering what lies in the ocean's depths or the vastness of space. Another important place needs to be explored as deeply as possible but is often neglected. This place is the vast world within you. So, in this chapter, you'll take a deep dive within yourself and explore terrain you never knew existed.

"Knowing yourself is true wisdom.".
Designed by freepik. Source: https://www.freepik.com/free-photo/medium-shot-human-silhouette-nature_38689099.htm

What's the point in being a know-it-all if you know everything except who you are? What's the point in gathering all this information only to let it go to waste because you're not using it? This chapter will be very practical, so if you intend to make the most of it, set aside whatever you're doing and give it your full attention. Otherwise, you may want to pick a different time when you can give this your full attention and practice what you'll learn here.

Why You Should "Know Thyself"

Why should you take time to know yourself? If the story of your life is feeling lost, confused, helpless, and hopeless, then knowing the power you carry within is the first step to setting yourself free from a life full of experiences that do not fulfill you.

There's not one person on the planet who doesn't feel the call to explore themselves. Everyone has a latent instinctive understanding that true power lies within, but this terrifies so many that they'd rather look for substitutes than the real thing.

So, they observe how other people who embody their inner power behave and attempt to copy that. Rather than adopt the state of being, they mimic it. Some try to make up for their lack of awareness of this power and how to wield it by going after power, money, and sensual pleasures. Sooner or later, they realize that those things must pale compared to the treasures within. If you can relate to this, then be glad you have been led to this book, this chapter, and this very moment.

You cannot solve the complex problems of life by imitating others without the energy that fuels their behavior and gives them their results. You won't find any satisfaction in seeking external validation either. True power comes from a place of authenticity, and you can't be authentic if you don't know who you are or what you're here for.

You have to deliberately look inside yourself to get to know the beautiful, the ugly, and the in-betweens, accepting them as the perfection of your being. The knowledge you have of yourself will be your compass, guiding you towards your True North to a fulfilling life that leaves an impact for the better.

If you choose to mimic others, you come from a place of inauthenticity. You're admitting that you don't have the power within you. You'll feel disconnected from your life and have a profound sense of emptiness that won't let you go. Copying others means putting on masks, makeup, and costumes, which can be very heavy and ill-fitting.

You did not incarnate into this existence to be a replica of another person in terms of self-expression and creativity. Everyone is an individual. You must find what makes you truly you and then express that. If you prefer to be a professional mimic, you not only concede your power to others but also limit your potential. That's not what you want.

True power comes from a place of authenticity.
Designed by freepik. *https://www.freepik.com/free-photo/full-shot-super-woman-with-superpowers_38170134.htm*

You want the clarity that comes with knowing your inner power. When you know what your values are and where your passions lie, these things are a beacon calling you toward the next step of your enlightenment. You proceed toward your dreams and goals confidently because you trust in the power you carry within. Your authenticity is undeniable and attractive to others who are like you.

Quantum Principles and Becoming Aware of Yourself

All things in the world are interconnected, and you're a part of it all. Would you believe a grain of sand in your hand holds the entire blueprint for existence? Well, as illogical as that might seem, it does, and so do you. As you've already learned, in the quantum world, particles exist in multiple states simultaneously. They have an effect on one another regardless of their distance, and they're also affected by an observer whose presence causes a change in their states by wave function collapse.

On the surface, it may seem none of these things have anything to do with your personal journey or becoming more self-aware, but that's not the case. Consider superposition and the infinite sea of possibilities available to you. Just as a particle exists in more than one state at the same time, so are you full of a myriad of possibilities within.

There's a cosmic buffet of options available to you, with every item yours for the taking. The key to expressing a specific version of yourself, therefore, is to turn your attention to it. As the observer of this different version of your life, you cause a wave function collapse that allows you to break past your limiting beliefs about what's possible for you and express yourself as this new, more expansive being.

What about quantum entanglement and what it says about everything being interconnected, no matter how far apart? This is an excellent metaphor for the connection you share with the world around you and the people in it. Recognize that you and everyone else are part of a collective or a body. If you cut your toe on a sharp rock, it needs to heal. Would you not dress the wound to help it? Would you say, "My toe isn't me, so that's none of my business?" Of course not.

If you have a need or something you want to manifest, and you rely on others to make decisions that will bring you the desired results, here's what you need to understand: you and those people are interconnected. When you trust that they, as extensions of yourself, will fulfill your need, it's as good as done. Even if you find this hard to believe, your interactions with others will reflect your expectations. They will either meet your needs or confirm your doubts by not fulfilling them. In essence, you receive what you observe and assume to be true about others.

Your desires reflect your authentic self. They represent who you are. If you haven't done the work to figure out what you are about, what makes you tick, what makes your heart sing, and what is absolute drudgery, then you're full of everyone else's ideas but yours. You live a life led by the world outside of you, pulled this way and that, tossed and turned by the tides and currents of the ocean of life.

The problem is that the observer effect is always in action, which means if you continue giving your attention and energy to the things that don't represent your ideals or higher self, you'll get more of the same. The life of an unconscious creator is full of chaos and turmoil. You don't have to keep suffering that. By learning who you are, you develop a stronger awareness of your thoughts, beliefs, and feelings. Self-awareness gives you more control of your inner power, allowing you to take the rudder of your life and steer your ship where you want it to go.

Energy, Quanta, and Inner Power

It's time to talk about the threads that connect energy, quanta, and your inner power so you have the essential knowledge to help you connect with and express more of a higher consciousness in your daily life.

The universe is a collection of various kinds of energy. "Quanta" is a word that defines the building blocks that make up the universe. They are little packages of energy, waves, and ripples of the universal ocean of energies. It's easy to confuse the quanta for energy, which is a more generic term, but they're not really the same. Quanta refers to tiny packages of specific kinds of energy, such as matter or light.

Now, what is it that drives the feelings you have? What's the source of your thoughts and actions? It's your inner power. This power is an expression of universal energy which is found in everyone and everything in existence. It is the spark of divinity that spiritual traditions and religions speak of. With this understanding of your inner power, the question is, what's the connection between energy quanta and the power within you?

Remember, separation does not exist. That you can see space between you and another person does not mean that you are not intricately connected. You share a connection not just with other people but with life forms and your environment, whether it's natural or man-made. You are made of the same energy that expresses itself in many forms, *whether as a rock, a cat, or a light bulb!* This is a quantum mechanics concept. Experts in the field have proven time and time again that everything in the universe is nonlocal. This principle of nonlocality implies that regardless of how far away you perceive something or someone from yourself, you are still connected.

What's the connection between this and your ability to work with your inner power to manifest your desires and develop a more conscious connection with higher consciousness? Assume you have an old-school radio set. If you want to listen to a specific radio station, you have to turn the dial so it matches the frequency of that station. In the same way, when you align the energy within you to match your desire's frequency and the infinite storehouse of the universal energy, you lock in on the manifestation of your desire. Stay with that frequency, and soon, more and more things in your life will shift or change to match it.

It all begins by becoming aware of your beliefs, emotions, and thoughts. Many live assuming they have no say about how they feel or what they think, burdened by the lie that the mind is in charge of them. They don't realize the mind is a tool they can use.

Imagine a carpenter who says, *"I don't use my hammer. It uses me."* Unless what you want them to fix isn't that serious, you have deep enough pockets, and you're curious about what they meant by that absurd statement, you wouldn't hire them.

So, *use your tools.*

Your ability to feel, think, and act are tools. Your mind is a tool, not your master. If you doubt that, the next time you have a negative thought, put it on a proverbial stand and grill it with questions about its validity, presenting any and all evidence you can come up with to prove it isn't true. You'll be surprised at how quickly you'll dispose of that thought when you've finished.

Do this exercise with any longstanding beliefs, too. If you think those will be a little difficult to disprove, remember what a belief really is; a thought you've been thinking for long enough and often enough that you think it's true because it resonates with you. In other words, you've thought it long enough that you, your life experience, and the thought are now an energetic match.

To tune your dial to the frequency of your desires, you deliberately select thoughts and feelings that match them. It may not feel natural at first, but if you do it long enough, it will become a habit. From then on, you'll act in line with those new feelings and thoughts, and this will lead to tangible changes in your life that encourage you to keep going.

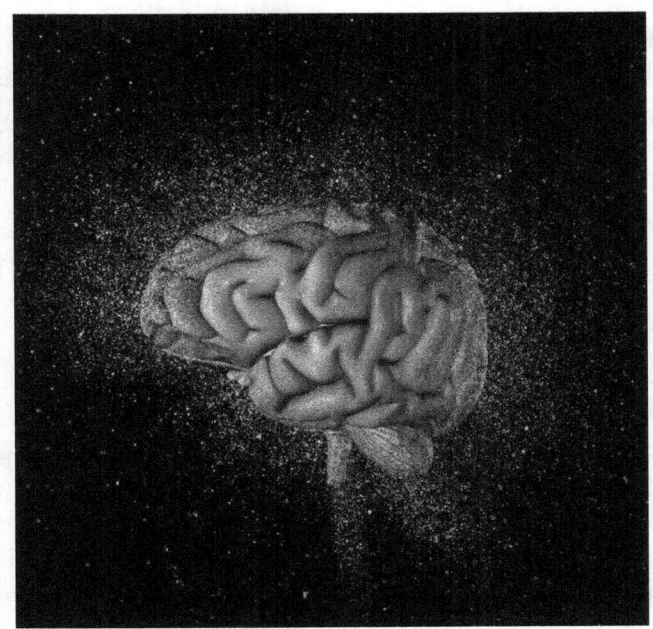

You control your mind, not the other way around.
Designed by freepik. https://www.freepik.com/free-photo/3d-render-brain-with-glitter-explosion-effect_987581.htm

As you evolve, you'll grow more aware of your thoughts, beliefs, and feelings. Keep your focus on your desires. Set a clear intention, and remind yourself of it as often as you can so you resonate with it. With time, this resonance will be obvious in your daily experience. Remember your unity with the universal energy in all this, and you'll see great results. The following are practical exercises to help you connect with the infinite power within you.

Practical Exercises to Tap into Your Inner Power

The Seed of Awareness Meditation

1. Find somewhere quiet and comfortable.
2. Sit upright, keeping your back straight, elongating your spine as if there's a rope connected to the top of your head, pulling you skyward.
3. Begin breathing deeply, taking your time with your inhales and exhaling until your lungs are empty. Keep your attention on what

your breath feels like as it enters and leaves your body.

4. While you meditate, thoughts will come to your mind and distract you from your breathing. This is completely natural. Acknowledge them when they arise, and don't judge them or identify with them.

5. Once you recognize that you have been distracted, feel gratitude that you noticed, and then turn your attention back to your breath. Do this as often as you are distracted, and never beat yourself up about it.

6. Sit in silent awareness of your breath for the next 10 to 15 minutes.

Use this simple meditation as a starting point for other practices that require going within. You'll have more powerful results this way than if you jump into other advanced meditations or visualization exercises like the next one. It works because it's like shutting the door on the physical world to become more conscious and aware of the spiritual realms within you.

Visualizing the World Within

1. Begin with your eyes closed. Become aware of your breath, like in the previous exercise. When you feel present and still, it's time to visualize.

2. In your imagination, imagine walking down a beautiful pathway toward the entrance of a magnificent garden. Notice the way your feet feel as you walk to the garden.

3. Enter the garden, and then stop just inside it. What do you see, hear, and smell? Pay attention to each of these things your senses pick up on, taking your time to study them. Maybe there's a babbling brook with gentle water sounds that put you at peace, an exquisite-looking bird flitting around, or an enchanting flower that draws you in.

4. Now, go further into the garden. Explore it, and notice the way you feel as you do. This garden is a reflection of your inner world. Note what it looks like, whether dreary and abandoned or flourishing and radiant.

5. As you explore, ask yourself what needs to change in your life to help you develop spiritually and become more of the person you'd like to be. If you haven't received an answer yet, don't

worry. You'll receive it another time, probably when you're in the middle of something mundane.

6. If your garden looks like it needs some love, you can touch the plants and imagine light flowing out of your palms to heal them.

7. Spend 5 to 10 minutes enjoying your garden's sights, sounds, and smells or tending to the parts that need love.

Firing Up an Energy Ball

1. After getting yourself into a meditative state, rub both palms together briskly for a few seconds until you feel the heat and tingle in them.

2. Now, pull your hands apart gradually until there are a few inches between them.

3. Pay attention to the feelings between them. It's a subtle energy.

4. In your mind's eye, imagine there's the energy between your palms as an actual ball of light.

5. Play with this energy by bringing your palms closer together and pulling them further apart than the first time. Feel the energy ball grow bigger and less subtle as you do this.

6. Now, imagine that as you keep bringing your palms together and apart, the energy becomes more intense each time.

7. Imagine changing the color of your energy ball, and then pay attention to the feelings that come up as you do this.

8. Now, bring your desired intention to mind. Keep your focus on your intention, and notice whether the ball's color and energetic feeling change to reflect your desire. Note that you must focus on this intention or desire as if it's already done, with a heart of gratitude.

9. Keep this energy ball between your hands for some minutes, soaking in its energy and enjoying the feeling.

10. When you are ready, bring the ball up to your face. With a deep, long breath, imagine you're inhaling the energy ball. Feel it go in through your nostrils, filling up your chest and then spreading its radiance through the rest of your body.

11. Now, see your body glowing inside and out with the light from this energy, pulsing brighter and brighter.

12. Offer thanks. You can keep it short and sweet with a simple "thank you" or spend more time being thankful for everything about your already fulfilled desire.

Seeing Auras

An aura is the energetic essence of a being, showing their current state of mind or general "energetic attitude." You can use auras to tell if there's something wrong with someone and they need help or if they mean you harm. For this exercise, you'll need a room that's not too bright but not poorly lit either. You also need someone else to help you here.

1. First, get into your meditative state.
2. When you feel centered, open your eyes and gaze at a solitary object in the room. Keep your gaze soft. You're not trying to penetrate it. Stare hard, and you'll strain your eyes and get no results.
3. When you've spent a few minutes staring at the object, slowly move your attention to the person whose aura you'll be seeing. Use your peripheral vision. Looking directly at them will keep you from seeing their aura.
4. Wait patiently. Initially, what you see may only be subtle, but with time and consistent practice, you'll see their aura with ease.

Discovering Your Power Animal

Your power animal is one of those beings assigned to you to help you through life. You can draw wisdom, guidance, knowledge, strength, and power from them. The following is a great exercise to help you learn who they are and connect with them from here on out. After meeting them, if you need their help with anything, you can also use this technique to revisit them and make your request. Here's how it works.

1. Once you've attained your centered, meditative state, imagine you're moving down into the Earth's core, passing by tree roots and rocks.
2. Imagine emerging from the Earth into the most beautiful, natural landscape you've ever seen.
3. While here, ask your power animal to reveal themselves to you, and thank them in advance for answering your call. Wait patiently, with a heart full of thanks and excitement.

4. When they appear, thank them for revealing themselves and for helping you navigate the ups and downs of your life. Ask for a deeper connection with them, and thank them once more.
5. When you're ready, imagine moving up into the sky, reencountering rocks and tree roots – and then emerging back into your body in your room.

These exercises aren't the only ones you can use to connect with higher consciousness and channel your inner power wherever you desire. There are many more out there if you do your research. Also, suppose you feel intuitively led to tweak these exercises or create your own. In that case, you should trust that hunch and develop your exercises.

You'll get the best results if you practice them daily, even if you can only afford five minutes each time. Consistency is the key to success here. If you don't get immediate results, or nothing happens the first few tries, that doesn't mean you've failed. Don't pressure yourself with expectations.

Instead, keep an open mind and keep up the practices. Think of them like brushing your teeth – you'll do that every day, whether or not you feel like it. Now you've learned how to "go within," you'll discover how to "go without."

Chapter 4: Go Beyond to Expand Your Awareness

"Whatever you come across, go beyond." – Nisargadatta Maharaj

You've learned to explore the worlds within you, but there's more to explore. Do you know you can travel from your body to worlds invisible to your physical eyes? Some of these worlds mimic the physical world closely, while others are so fantastical that it's difficult to imagine them if you've never been.

Astral projection and shamanic journeys are not the same.
Designed by freepik. https://www.freepik.com/free-photo/fantasy-astral-wallpaper-composition_39425682.htm

People confuse astral projection and shamanic journeys, thinking they're the same thing when they aren't. The only similarity they share is they're both metaphysical practices meant to put you in contact with worlds beyond the physical realm. In this chapter, you'll learn how to use them for spiritual exploration and connect with higher consciousness on a deeper level.

Shamanic Journeying

For many centuries, shamans have used shamanic journeying to explore all the realms of consciousness that are unavailable to the physical senses. On a shamanic journey, you can communicate with spiritual beings such as your power animals, spirit guides, and other entities.

On this journey, you are in a state of consciousness where you can receive information from various levels of reality. Sometimes, while the shaman travels, their body is temporarily inhabited by the spirits of benevolent beings who impart much-needed healing and information to those who need it.

Prepare your mental state before embarking on a journey. You need to have a clear reason for wanting to visit these other realms, so spend time setting your intention for each trip. It's also best to practice this in a space where you feel safe and secure. If you feel fear, you may attract low vibration, unwanted entities, and energies to you, which would disrupt your session.

There are several shamanic techniques you could use to get into a state of trance that allows you to connect with different levels of consciousness. If you struggle with a journey, you can enlist the help of your spirit guides, power animals, or other beings you believe in.

Benefits of Shamanic Journeying

Apart from how interesting it is to experience worlds other than your own, there are numerous benefits of practicing shamanic journeying.

. One of the most remarkable ways to draw on your inner power for healing is by using shamanic journeys. On your journey, you'll encounter guides who are knowledgeable in the healing arts and can diagnose the precise problems you're struggling with. They have experience beyond time that extends across all realms and will know what to recommend.

Sometimes, they'll act directly on your issue by sending healing energy into whatever part of your body requires it. The healing you receive from these beings is so profound that it also cleanses you of whatever negative, low vibrational energies led to your condition in the first place.

Here's a disclaimer. *You should see your medical doctor first whenever you have physical health issues or talk to a counselor or therapist if you're struggling mentally.* If you're still struggling to get better, then try shamanic journeying. You see, every problem in the physical world has a spiritual origin. There's no better way to address health issues than by working with higher consciousness in conjunction with the conventional help you receive from licensed, professional doctors and therapists.

Your Stress Level Will Decrease: Something about this metaphysical practice leaves practitioners feeling relaxed and at ease when they return to the physical world. They travel to other worlds full of peace and serenity and soak up the energy there. When you return from a trip, the reminder of the vastness of the cosmos makes your worries and concerns seem infinitesimally insignificant. The more you practice shamanic journeying, the easier it is for you to put life in perspective.

You'll Discover Who You Really Are: Many people today become what they've been told they should be rather than be their true selves. This is one of several reasons that people are mostly miserable. When you go on a shamanic journey, you will meet yourself – without all the frills and trimmings the world has put upon you. You'll learn much more about yourself than you could ever conceive through contemplation.

Some of the things you discover may seem unsettling at first, but keep an open mind. Self-discovery is always worth the time and energy. Once you learn more about your power, you can't go back to living a life weighed down by others' expectations about how you should behave. You know what's right for you and what isn't, and you are unfazed by any external pressure to get you to be something other than who you are.

You Solve the Most Difficult Problems You've Struggled with Your Whole Life: Is there a particular issue that has left you stumped for a long time? You think you've come up with the perfect solution, only to find that it all falls apart when you apply it. This failure has happened repeatedly, to the point where you've become disillusioned and are ready to give up. If you can relate to this, you should definitely try shamanic journeying.

With shamanic journeys, you can reach out to your personal guides and ask them to let you know where you're going wrong. They'll point out what you've been missing. They'll help you make the energy change to bring about the manifestation of the solution to this problem in a natural way.

Your Creativity Will Soar: On a shamanic journey, there is so much to explore, not just with what you feel and experience with your spiritual senses but also with your interpretation of those experiences. The vastness of the shamanic realms and how they express themselves is more than enough material from which to draw inspiration.

Regardless of your field of work, whether in the arts or some other industry not typically considered creative, you will find inspirational ideas to help you thrive. All you have to do is reach out to your guide and ask them to share what you need to know.

The Three Realms

In shamanic traditions, the cosmos has split into three distinct realms:
- The Lower Realm
- The Middle Realm
- The Upper Realm

In some traditions, you'll find these three worlds are divided further into subworlds, but generally speaking, you encounter only three roads on your shamanic trance journey. You could travel to these worlds independently, but it's more usual to be accompanied by your spirit guide or power animal.

In shamanic traditions, the cosmos has split into three distinct realms.
Designed by freepik. https://www.freepik.com/free-photo/glowing-satellite-orbits-planet-star-filled-galaxy-generated-by-ai_40968223.htm

The Lower Realm: Most travel to the lower world the first time they go on a shamanic journey. To get there, you'd have to descend into the earth using the World Tree, which is also called the Axis Mundi. This spiritual tree gives you access to all three worlds. You travel by moving through its trunk.

When making your way into the lower world, you have to go through a long corridor or tunnel, which you enter through the hole or opening in the earth. The hole could be one made by an animal, a waterfall opening, or a slit at the bottom of a tree trunk. It could also be a staircase that leads you down. However, the entrance to this world presents itself, and you will be entering the earth to get to the lower world.

The lower world is the realm of transformational power. In this world, your helper will be in the form of a power animal. However, other helpers could take the form of wind, trees, and other elements of nature. They could also be your ancestors, too. They'll appear in a way that resonates with you.

If you wish to enjoy your shamanic journeys, develop a relationship with these guides. The more time and effort you put into establishing a strong connection between you, the easier it will be to explore the shamanic realms and gain whatever you need from them.

The lower world is where you'll go if you need healing, transformation, and power in your life. The power you receive here will help you not only in your work but also in your spiritual development. This world is a representation of your inner psyche or subconscious mind. So, in a sense, it's not really about "going beyond" or "going without," but going within.

The Middle Realm: This middle world closely mirrors the earthly world but has everything to do with spiritual dimensions and the soul. Think of it like the earth as you know it but with an overlay of spiritual beings and structures. It's like pulling back the veil to see more of what's present in you that often goes undetected in the physical world. This is where you discover nature, creatures, and the different souls that make up nature itself, like the souls of pets, weather, trees, mountains, land, etc. It contains the present, past, and future of life on earth.

Is there something specific you'd like to know about some event? Do you want to gather information about a particular area? In that case, you should journey to the Middle Realm. From here, you can work alongside the soul of a specific place on earth or in nature. Every ritual practiced in different spiritual traditions and cultures involves drawing power from this world.

The Upper World: This is the world that sits above the Earth. You gain access to it by journeying into space and going beyond the stars. You can tell the difference between the upper and middle worlds by the difference in vibration if you're sensitive enough to pick up on it. The upper world vibrates at a distinctly different frequency from the lower one. This difference in vibration is also mirrored in the sort of assistance you can expect from either of these worlds.

For instance, if you want a higher perspective on your life and you want to find the space between yourself and a difficult situation that has overwhelmed you, you would be best served by going to the upper world. Also, if you'd like to discover new parts of yourself and ways to express your creativity, the upper world is where you should be.

You have two options when it comes to journeying to the Upper Realm. You could make your way higher and higher to the place beyond the stars through the Axis Mundi, or you could descend into the depths of the lower world and continue your descent until you emerge in the upper world itself. This is possible because these three realms are interconnected with one another. It's a cyclical route.

How to Go on a Shamanic Journey

1. Get ready by finding a quiet space free from distractions and disturbances. You should feel safe and secure in this space.
2. Select your world. While nothing stops you from visiting the Lower Realm, seeing the Middle and Upper Realms may be more beneficial. If you're eventually led by your guides to visit the Lower Realm, then you can rely on them to get you there.
3. Decide what your intention is for this shamanic journey. Do you want healing? Do you seek clarity on a confusing matter? Would you simply like to get to know your guides? Whatever it is you want to do, get clear about it and fix it in your mind.
4. Begin drumming. If you don't have a drum, you can listen to shamanic drumming music for free on the Internet. If you find that too distracting, you can listen to your heartbeat. The point is to pay attention to a repetitive sound that is constant enough to cause you to enter a trance state.

5. Picture a great tree before you. This is the Axis Mundi that connects you to the different realms. Find the slit at the base of the tree and enter it, remembering to keep your destination firmly in mind as you walk down the corridor toward the other side.
6. In the Middle Realm, explore the world around you with your intention in mind. You can also intend for your guide to show up and offer you whatever you seek or lead you to it. Don't be afraid to ask questions, engage with the entities you encounter, and observe the world around you.
7. If your intention is to reach the Upper Realm, find the Axis Mundi and climb it until you're up in the stars, and keep going until you're beyond them. Alternatively, ask your guide to take you there, and you'll both fly to that realm beyond the stars.
8. Once in the Upper Realm, remember to engage with guides, beings, and the world around you with your intention in mind.
9. To make your way back to the physical world, retrace your steps. As you emerge from the Axis Mundi, your awareness returns to your body in your safe space.
10. Take some time to breathe deeply, grounding yourself in your body by increasing your awareness of it. When you feel fully present, open your eyes.
11. Journal about your experiences, new perceptions you received, and any new questions that have sprung up that you can address on your next journey.

Astral Projection

Astral projection is also called astral travel. When you go on this sort of journey, you're having an out-of-body experience or OOBE. Astral travel is a metaphysical process of transporting your consciousness out of your physical body and onto other planes of existence. Some say you're not moving your consciousness from your physical body to your astral one but only changing to your astral consciousness. However you want to describe it, you can astral project through visualization, meditation, lucid dreaming, and more.

When astral projecting, you'll notice all sorts of sensations from the moment you become aware that you are awake to when you actually leave your body. Astral projection will completely change the way you look at the world. When your astral body detaches from your physical one, you will realize that there is no end to life and no reason to be afraid of death when it comes.

Some people have the erroneous belief that astral projection is dangerous because it's possible never to be able to return to your body. Some say some other entity could possess your body while you're gone, but that's not true. Your body's yours, and no one has permission to eject you from it. Also, one of your main challenges will be staying out of your body as long as possible. Simply thinking about your body or feeling for it is enough to return you to the physical world, and there's a silver cord that keeps you tethered to your physical body.

If you want to succeed with this spiritual practice, it's better not to discuss it with skeptics until you've done it. No matter how stoic you are or how strong your will is, skepticism could be counterproductive to you making your first journey into the astral plane. Fear and doubt are the two most troublesome roadblocks to successfully projecting your consciousness from the physical realm to other planes, so do what you can to avoid them at all costs.

Here are some of the benefits of astral projection:

1. You can meet spiritual guides who'll offer insightful information about where you are in life.
2. You can use this realm to get inspiration for your projects in life. For instance, you could conjure up paintings, musical pieces, ideas for architecture, etc. The possibilities are endless.
3. In the astral realm, you can role-play what it would be like to live as the person you prefer to be. This will give you a clear picture of what it means to have manifested your dreams and make it easier and faster for those things to become physical.
4. You'll get rid of your fear of death once you practice leaving your body.
5. Astral projection causes you to become more self-aware, which is excellent for spiritual development.
6. Speaking of spiritual developments, the more you astral project, the more you'll experience anomalies in life that show you how plastic reality is, making it easier to create what you want in life.

7. You'll experience synchronicity and the awakening of various psychic abilities that you're unaware of or haven't been able to use to your fullest potential.

How to Practice Astral Projection

Get Your Mind and Body Ready: If you want to project your consciousness to the astral plane successfully, you have to learn how to relax while simultaneously concentrating on your goal. Therefore, you should be in an environment that's safe, calm, and free from distractions. Meditating before your astral projection practice will give you better results.

You also have to release your fears. Astral projection is a practice that has existed for centuries and is perfectly safe. You won't lose access to your body because you're always tethered to it by a silver cord, which you may or may not see during your travels.

Before you begin, make sure you are in a comfortable position. Sit in an upright position or lie down. If you choose to lie down, beware that you may fall asleep before you successfully leave your body.

If you find sitting in an upright position uncomfortable, you could use a recliner or stack some pillows behind your back to imitate one. Make sure your body is clean and clear of drugs. Any depressants or stimulants could interfere with your goal and make it hard to leave your body – and that includes coffee and cigarettes.

Close Your Eyes, Breathe Properly, and Relax: You should take diaphragmatic breaths, meaning your stomach should rise with every inhale, and your lungs should be completely empty on your exhales. As you focus on your breath, you'll feel more relaxed. Try inhaling through your nose for four seconds, holding that breath for seven seconds, and then exhaling through your slightly parted lips for eight seconds.

Wait for the Vibrations: While you wait, resist the urge to move. Your mind will test you to see if you're awake because you're in such a relaxed state that it's as if you're asleep. It will send signals to your body to get you to turn over or scratch an itch. If you ignore these signals, your mind will assume that your body is asleep, putting you in a state of sleep paralysis, which is meant to prevent you from acting out your dreams.

In this state, you may begin to notice your body vibrating. It feels like intense currents of electricity flowing through you, but it's not painful. You can control the vibrations if you want by moving them around.

Don't be surprised if you start noticing sounds like voices or laughter. It may also feel as if there are other presences with you in the room, but there is nothing to be afraid of. No matter what's happening around you, remember that you are safe. Don't be in a hurry to move to the next step. Take time to feel the vibrations.

Imagine a Rope Above Your Head: Keep your attention on this dangling rope for a while. Then, imagine reaching out of your physical body with your astral hands to grab onto the rope. Once the rope is firmly in your astral hands, pull on it to lift your astral body out of your physical one. You'll have a brief sensation of being in two bodies at once, so focus on using your astral senses rather than your physical ones. Continue pulling until you are fully out of your body.

Move to the Furthest Section of Your Room: From here, you can take a look at your body while sleeping in bed. Whatever you do, don't get excited or scared, as these intense emotions can yank you back into your body.

Leave Your Room: You could use the door if you wish, but being in your astral body means you can easily pass through solid materials. So, if you want to walk through walls to get to the outside of your house, you can do that. If you'd like to test what it's like to fly, gently tap the floor with a foot to bounce yourself into the air and then move through the ceiling up into the sky. With your mind alone, you can propel yourself in any direction at any speed you like.

Explore Your Neighborhood, Town, Country, and Continent: Since you're in your astral form, you don't need to adhere to the idea of taking time to move through space to get from one location to another. So, if you're in Cape Town, South Africa, and you'd like to be in Paris, you could get there by picturing or visualizing the Eiffel Tower or any other Parisian landmark that you know of. Even if you don't have a landmark in mind, the intention to be in Paris is enough to get you there instantly.

Go Beyond the Earth's Orbit: Nothing is keeping you from exploring beyond the Earth. To experience yourself as being truly connected to the universe, you should make your way into outer space, toward the stars and beyond them. You don't need to know what lies beyond to get there. Simply intend that this is where you'd like to go. You'll find the astral plane is very receptive and highly affected by your intentions, emotions, and expectations.

Seek Your Spirit Guide and Ask Them Whatever You Desire: Again, all you have to do is intend to meet with them. In the astral plane, you do not have to communicate with spoken words. You may use telepathy and receive blocks of thought that contain vast information from your guides.

Return to Your Body: To do this, simply think about your sleeping form on the bed or feel it, and you'll be there. Before you return, state firmly and aloud to yourself that you will remember everything you have experienced. This is a crucial step to downloading the information you've received instead of forgetting it once you wake up.

As you merge with your body, make a loud sound like a roar or a scream to help you connect your astral and physical consciousnesses. In this way, you are more likely to remember everything you learned on your journey.

Now that you know how to go within and go without, what's next? It's only logical that you meet your higher self, isn't it? Find out how to do just that in the next chapter.

Chapter 5: Meet Your Higher Self

"Sometimes your Higher Self will guide you to make mistakes so you can learn lessons." - Gabrielle Bernstein

It's time to get to know your higher self. Once you do this, your life will be radically transformed. You'll wonder why you didn't look into this sooner than now, but better late than never, right?

Let yourself be your guide.
Designed by freepik. https://www.freepik.com/free-vector/gradient-surrealist-galaxy-illustration_45199603.htm

Your Higher Self

The idea of the higher self is familiar to many spiritual traditions. Some call it the I Am. Others call it the Authentic Self. You may call it the divine self, the mind, Christ consciousness, full potential self, fully realized self, universal consciousness, cosmic consciousness, soul, or self. Whatever title you choose, it represents a grander, greater aspect of you than you are currently embodying or capable of grasping right now.

As your higher self, you express love in its truest form. The love you share for yourself and others has nothing to do with ego. You could say your higher self is love itself. From the perspective of your divine self, you do not see any flaws in anything or anyone because you deem it all divinely perfect. This self never judges anything as evil and also does not acknowledge separation. Through these divine eyes, all things are emanations of the Creator. Your self is a beacon, a light that guides you back home to the unity of consciousness. It is infinite wisdom, love, and light.

It's possible to embody your higher self in your everyday life. Remember the quantum principle of superposition. As particles exist in multiple states, you can express your egoic self and hire yourself simultaneously for a richer, more rewarding life. What about entanglement? No matter how dark things may seem or how long it's been since you've given thought to the subject, your higher self will always be connected to you. If you're not aware of that connection, it's only because you have not put in the work to become conscious of it. This entanglement between you and the grander version of your being will make itself more evident when you deliberately reach out to connect to it.

By turning your attention towards your higher self, you activate the observer effect for good in your life. You cause your way of being to change for the better, to mirror this version of yourself that is perfection and love.

Benefits of Connecting with Your Higher Self

What are the benefits you'll enjoy when you connect with your higher self and live with its consciousness daily?

You'll Experience an Increase in Clarity: By tuning in with this version of yourself, you'll no longer be bogged down by confusion or the feeling of being lost.

Your Ability to Focus on What Matters Will Improve: By keeping your awareness tethered to the cosmic and spiritual version of yourself, you'll find that you have no problems focusing on the things that matter the most.

Embodying Your Higher Self Leads to More Mindfulness: Mindfulness means being grounded in the present. You'll no longer be bogged down by what happened in the past or what may come in the future. From this perspective, you'll finally understand what Jesus Christ meant when he said in the book of Matthew, chapter 6, verse 34, *"Take therefore no thought for the morrow; for the morrow shall take thought for the things of itself. Sufficient for the day is its own trouble."*

You'll Have More Respect and Compassion For Yourself: Since your higher self is incapable of perceiving anything as imperfect or wrong, you, too, will emulate that quality. This compassion and respect will also extend to others in your life. You'll learn to value everyone, regardless of where they're at or what they're struggling with.

Your Mental and Physical Health Will Improve: Connecting with your higher self means allowing more of the natural creative energy that sustains the world to flow through you. If you constantly deal with depression and stress, you'll find this connection helps you feel better – in addition to therapy, of course.

Cultural and Spiritual Perspectives on the Higher Self

There are many interpretations of the higher self across cultures and traditions. In the West, the higher self refers to you as a person but at your most spiritually evolved. You express uncommon wisdom, and your love is pure and unconditional compared to most. This statement is not an egoic thing, and there is no competition or pride. You are simply a being who resonates with these ideas. According to the Western perception of this idea, the true self is who you are when you are self-expressive and self-directed. As this person, you don't give in to the desires of the masses because you prefer to be independent.

Connecting to your higher self means shedding ego narratives about yourself. Designed by freepik. https://www.freepik.com/free-vector/gradient-surrealist-galaxy-illustration_45183518.htm

In Native American cultures, the people value being interdependent with one another, seeing that way of life as superior to the prevalent hyper-independence celebrated in modern times. So, their perspective on the higher self involves community. It is about honoring the threads that connect one and all in life. Therefore, in these cultures (and tribal ones), the higher self is the sum of these connections.

Spiritual traditions from the East view the higher self as your true essence. It's you with no limitations. As your higher self, you've surpassed egoic attachments. It's not separate from you but a key part of who you are that is still connected to the universal consciousness or infinite intelligence. To grow more connected to this self, shed all the layers of unnecessary things that the ego has piled upon your soul. In other words, strip yourself of everything you've assumed you are because they keep you from discovering your true essence.

Stories About Connecting with Higher Self

"My higher self loves to connect with me using synchronicities. Sometimes, she'll also speak to me with oracle or tarot cards. I remember this one time when I had a personal issue I was dealing with, and I cried a lot about it. Suddenly, I began seeing angel numbers popping up everywhere, and I'm very certain it was my trying to comfort me. The first time I met her during meditation, I was simply stunned by her beautiful energy.

She helps me out whenever I need to do work with crystals by choosing the correct ones for my needs. One thing she told me that I have taken to heart is that I shouldn't take life too seriously and instead, I should look at everything through a child's eyes." - Fatima

"I remember when I had begun meditating every day for 10 minutes. My desire to learn more about my spiritual life led me to discover a few videos on YouTube about how to connect with my higher self. One of the videos, in particular, called to me. I tried the exercise it suggested and left it at that. It took two months after four of my higher selves to make themselves fully known. When we established contact with each other, the feeling was intense. After that day, I noticed I pick up on their messages more clearly than ever." - Vincent

"Ever since I connected with my higher self, I have been experiencing miracle after miracle. Usually, these miracles start as seeming devastation or something to despair over, but things turn around for the better every time. My higher self has been teaching me that there's no reason to panic just because something bad appears to be happening. He has shown me that if I remain neutral or even positive in the face of these things, they will be transmuted into a better situation than before those events happened. The love I feel for the world and myself is so deep that sometimes I cry, especially in large crowds. The crazy part is that others cry along with me, like they know me and are glad to reconnect with me. I'm also experiencing telepathic communication." - Zach

Do you feel inspired by these stories? There's no reason you can't have stories of your own. Take time to reflect on different moments in your life where you felt as if there was a higher power intervening or offering you guidance. For instance, was there a time when you felt strongly about something, and it turned out to be correct? That was your higher self in action. If you've ever felt intense peace and clarity even when things were not working out or appeared to be confusing, this is because your higher self fueled you with resilience.

What about your dreams? Are there any that stand out in particular? Do you recall meeting someone who felt like a teacher or a guide? Have you had any visions that revealed to you what you needed to do about a situation in your life? These messages come from your higher self as well.

Your higher self can use synchronicities of events and numbers to get your attention. Designed by freepik.
https://www.freepik.com/free-photo/numerology-concept-composition_38110409.htm

Don't dismiss synchronicities. In the real sense of it, there's no such thing as a coincidence. Someone else may claim you're only noticing coincidences, but synchronicity is more than that, as a string of events plays out in a way that holds deep meaning for you. Your higher self can use synchronicities of events and numbers to get your attention.

Higher Self Meditation

This excellent meditation will help you connect with your higher self. To perform this meditation, you'll need to tune into your third eye and crown chakras, which are energy centers that allow information and energy to flow into and out of your body and spirit. Your third eye chakra is on your forehead, slightly above and directly between both eyebrows, while your crown chakra is at the top of your head in the middle. Here are the instructions for this meditation.

1. Perform your basic meditation until you get to a serene state of mind.
2. Ground yourself by imagining roots that come out from the base of your spine and go down into the depths of the earth. Feel the stability and support these roots offer you.
3. Move your attention to your third eye chakra. Imagine an indigo light pulsing in this area. See it become brighter on each inhale,

and as you exhale, imagine the light spreading through your body. Spend a few minutes doing this.

4. Now, move your attention to your crown chakra. Imagine a radiant white or violet light pulsing in this area. With each inhale, let the light grow brighter. With each breath, let the light flood your body inside and out.

5. Imagine a beam of white light that begins from your third eye chakra, moves up through your crown chakra, and towards the sky into the universe. This is the light that connects you to your higher self. Feel their energy flowing through you, full of love, wisdom, and guidance. Feel this energy flow in through your crown chakra and your third eye chakra and radiate through your body. Remain here as long as you like.

6. When you're done, imagine that the light beam from the sky gently retracts into your ground chakra and disappears. See the light in both chakras slowly dimming and returning to their regular state. After a few more deep breaths to ground yourself in your body, you may open your eyes slowly.

If you would like to connect with your higher self through shamanic journeying or astral projection, you can do this. All you need to do is be clear about your intention before you begin those practices, and when you are in that altered state or different realm, request their presence.

5 Tips for Connecting with Your Higher Self

1. Spend less time looking at screens and more time in nature or meditation.

2. Practice journaling daily to become more self-aware and track the different ways your higher self has made themselves known in your life.

3. Spend time contemplating your soul's purpose. If you've already worked it out, contemplate the different ways you could continue to pursue it.

4. Decide to trust your intuition with no questions asked. The more you trust it instead of leaning on your logic alone, the more accurate it will become with time.

5. Be consistent in all your spiritual practices. You'll have far more results if you do them every day than if you do them once every

couple of weeks or months.

Now you know all there is to know about your higher self, it's time to discover how you can work with spirit guides.

Chapter 6: Work with Spirit Guides

"Your Spirit Guides and Angels will never let you down as you build a rapport with them. In the end, they may be the only ones who don't let you down."

– Linda Deir

Spirit guides are divine entities assigned to guide and protect you throughout your life. You didn't arrive on the planet on your own. You know you have an entire team supporting and caring for you. They would do so much more for you if you would only acknowledge them and ask for their help because they respect free will and will not act unless asked.

Spirit guides can show up in the form of animals, among many other forms.
Designed by freepik. https://www.pexels.com/photo/white-and-black-wolf-397857/

Your spirit guides act as protectors, keeping you safe from dangerous situations. They are the best mentors who can guide you through the different issues of life, from business and finances to health and relationships, etc. This is because they have a strong connection to infinite intelligence and can offer you divine wisdom when you ask for it.

There's no limit to the forms that spirit guides can take to interact with you. It all depends on what your spiritual preconceptions and beliefs are, as well as the experiences you've had. Sometimes, they can show up as animals. At other times, they could be your angels, ancestors, or beings from other dimensions.

It should feel comforting to know that you always have a spiritual team at your disposal to help you remain conscious of higher consciousness and connected to your higher self. Your spirit guides are benevolent. There's no such thing as asking them for too much.

Where are these guides exactly? These beings dwell in realms that aren't physical. They operate through energy and vibration that's on the same frequency as the spirit world, which means if you desire to experience them more fully and connect with them daily, you should grow your spiritual muscles. Your daily practice with meditation, contemplation, and other spiritual practices will help you get to the point where you can easily connect with your spirit guides whenever you want without having to get into a meditative state.

Spirit guides play an essential role, acting as the bridge between the physical and the spiritual. If you struggle to progress in your spiritual journey by calling upon them for assistance, you'll be amazed at how much further you'll go. They'll help you discover the blocks in your life that keep you from accessing spiritual growth and dissolve them on your behalf, with your consent.

In other words, you don't have to settle for simply asking them what you need to change about yourself. You can also ask them for the energy and will to implement their suggestions, and you'll inexplicably drop habits that had always been hard to quit, picking up new ones that serve your highest good. Your spirit guides can help you discover your inner power and offer you information and knowledge that is not accessible to the ordinary person or obtainable through regular means.

If you've decided you'd consciously like to work with them, then you must build an attitude of trust and surrender. For too long, people have labored under the misguided notion that they must travel the journey of life on their own, and this makes things needlessly harder. Working with your spirit guides means letting go of this idea. Release your need to be in control. Slide over to the passenger seat and allow your guides to take the wheel. For best results, don't be a backseat driver.

If you need help to develop your intuition or improve your psychic abilities, your guides will help you. They'll help you become more sensitive to the subtle energies around you every day, and that can be very useful in navigating your daily life with others. So don't be afraid to ask them for their assistance and prepare for levels of awareness like nothing you've experienced.

Types of Spirit Guides

Animal Guides: These guides are also known as animal spirits or power animals. Each one has a unique set of attributes depending on what animal they are since different animals symbolize different things. For instance, an eagle could represent vision, a bear could represent introspection and strength, and a butterfly could represent growth and transformation. Rather than rely only on generic interpretations of what each animal means, check in with your intuition. What does this animal represent to you? That's how you'll make the most of your connection to it.

Ancestors: Ancestors are the spirits of those connected to you by blood. The wisdom and guidance they offer you come from the collective experiences of their lives. Your ancestors are familiar with the challenges you face and the ones your bloodline, in particular, has struggled with.

Your ancestors could be people you've known from your past or those who passed on before you were born and had the chance to interact with them. For the most part, they have your best interests at heart, but if you choose to interact with them, you should specify that you only want to interact with those ancestors who truly care about your highest good. Why is this necessary? Well, imagine having Ted Bundy as an ancestor. Exactly.

Ascended Masters: These are highly evolved beings who have achieved enlightenment, having experienced multiple lifetimes – and learned so much from their travels. Jesus, Quan Yin, and Buddha are just a few of the most popular Ascended Masters. Not only have they had experience living on Earth, but they've also evolved on other spiritual dimensions. They've achieved unity with higher consciousness but choose to offer help and guidance to as many as call out to them.

Angels: Angels are celestial beings whose job is to guide you down the right path and keep you safe. There are various kinds of angels, but the most popular are the archangels. These are the angels who have specific qualities they're known for. For instance, Archangel Michael is typically called upon when one needs protection or strength. If you would like to be more creative and communicate better, then Archangel Gabriel is the best being to call upon. You can reach out to these beings or have them connect with you through your dreams, visions, and intuition.

Angels are spirit guides as well.
Designed by freepik. https://www.pexels.com/photo/stone-sculpture-of-an-angel-with-a-book-against-clouded-sky-8592167/

Nature Spirits: These spirits are responsible for the natural world. They have a profound connection with everything to do with nature and work hard to ensure all of life remains in perfect ecological balance. These are the spirits of the elements like fire, water, air, and earth – as well as of plants, rocks, mountains, etc.

This is by no means an exhaustive list of the different kinds of guides available to help you. If you need more information on who your guides are, you can always ask them, and they will tell you everything you need to know.

How to Connect with Your Spirit Guides

There are multiple ways to connect with your spirit guides. If you've never had any supernatural experience before that would suggest that they exist, you don't have to wait for them to reach out to you first. You could be the one to initiate contact. These are the various ways to establish a rapport with your guides.

Using Meditation: You already know the basics of how to meditate. So, if you'd like to use meditation as a tool to connect you with your spirit guide, set an intention before you begin the process. Don't be dismayed if nothing happens after the first try. Continue your meditation practice with your intention front and center in your mind, and sooner or later, they'll make themselves known in the best way and at the best time.

Through Dreams and Visions: Dreams are an excellent way to establish contact with your spirit guides. For some, seeing physical manifestations of spiritual phenomena is a little too scary. Your dreams are the perfect setting for a meeting between you and your spirit guides. This is because you already expect strange things to happen in dreams, as a rule. So, it won't freak you out too much if certain beings approach you in a dream and let you know that they are your guides.

Do you want to connect with your guides through dreams? In that case, you should set the intention before you go to bed every night and also keep a journal beside you. As soon as you awaken from your dream, write down whatever it is they shared with you so you don't forget, and you can reflect upon the message later.

If you are clairvoyant or have some activity with your third eye chakra, you may also experience visions. Think of these visions as being similar to dreams, except they take place during your waking state. They could be as short as a quick flash or as long as your guides need to get their message across to you.

Signs and Synchronicities: Your spirit guides will send you specific signals, which could be in the form of notable events or unusual phenomena around you, to let you know that there's something more going on or that they are present. The signs could be patterns of events that repeat themselves, a gut feeling, or an intuitive nudge. The science could also come in the form of goosebumps, vibrations in your body, and a sudden sense of "knowing" the truth.

As for meaningful coincidences or synchronicities, they are excellent tools to help you become alert to the spirit world and the presence of your guides. Remember, when it comes to synchronistic events, their importance or significance lies in their meaning, not cause and effect. Synchronicity can play out in the form of angel numbers you see all around you. You could be thinking about your brother-in-law and suddenly get a call from him.

Maybe there's a big decision you have to make, and you're feeling confused about whether or not to act. Then you suddenly stumble upon a forgotten book on a bench, with a highlighted sentence on its open page that addresses exactly what you need to know.

Every time you receive these signs and synchronicities, pause and acknowledge them. Thank your guides for reaching out to you, and ask them to communicate with you in even clearer ways if you're feeling lost and confused about what they mean.

To maintain the flow of information between you and your spirit guides through signs and synchronicities, you should journal daily. Also, get into the habit of meditating whenever you notice these signs, especially if there is time and you have privacy. Set the intention to have these messages become clearer each time, and you will no longer question what they're trying to tell you.

Automatic Writing and Channeling: Your guides can communicate to you through automatic writing, which is a practice in which you get into a meditative state and then, prepared with your pen and paper or word processor, write down whatever flows through you without any thought. Channeling is the same as automatic writing, with the difference being that you speak your guides' messages rather than writing them down. Some of the most famous channelers known to the spiritual community are Esther Hicks, Darryl Anka, and Jane Roberts.

If you would like to practice automatic writing, get your writing tools prepared first. Next, set your intention to communicate with your spirit guides. Following that, begin your meditation, keeping your focus on your intention. When you feel still and centered, you can begin writing. Resist the temptation to try to understand what's flowing out of you. Even if the beginning appears nonsensical, trust that it will eventually have meaning, or the meaning will be revealed to you later when you review your notes.

If you choose to channel, you will do the same thing as with automatic writing. Prepare a recording app or device to record everything that you're going to say. Set your intention to communicate with your spirit guides, then enter into your meditative state. Once you're feeling centered, begin to speak as you are led. Once more, what comes through you doesn't have to make sense. The more you practice this, the better you get at picking up on the energetic impressions from your spirit guides and interpreting them accurately. You'll have less and less of your ego tainting their messages with its biases and assumptions.

Divination: Divination is a metaphysical practice that involves discovering what will happen in the future or discerning what's going on now or in the past. It is picking up on information that would be impossible to access through ordinary means. You can use several divination tools to connect with your spirit guide if that's your desire. You could use runes, tarot cards, pendulums, etc. Before using your chosen tool, use meditation to ground and center yourself, set your intention, and then begin your work.

You can use tarot cards to connect with your spirit guides.
Designed by freepik. https://www.freepik.com/free-photo/high-angle-woman-reading-tarot-home_39886546.htm

Tarot cards come with pictures and text to let you know what each card means. You use them by shuffling them while thinking of the question you want to ask or asking it aloud. Then, you either keep shuffling until a card flies out of the deck, or you set the deck down and pick a card from wherever you're intuitively led. Apply the card's meaning to your question, and you'll have your answer. If it's not clear, ask aloud for clarification, shuffle the deck once more, and then select another card. This new card will offer more insight from your guides, clarifying the first answer.

Runes have their meanings, too. You only need to study what each implies, cast them, and read the answers from your guides. Pendulums are excellent for receiving yes or no answers to your questions, so consider studying how those work and investing in a good one for your practice.

Tips to Facilitate Communication with Your Guides

1. Keep a journal of all the messages you've received and the questions you have for your guides.
2. Commit to trusting your intuition, and you'll get better at telling it apart from your regular thoughts and feelings daily.
3. Keep the space where you connect with your spirit guides sacred. If you can't for some reason, then whenever you're about to practice, you should envision a white light that clears out all negative, stale energies in the room before you start.
4. Learn to be patient. Learning to communicate with your spirit guide is not a one-day affair.
5. Ask them to give you signs and guide you whenever you can.

You know everything there is to know about how to connect with your spirit guides. Does the thought of exploring different timelines interest you? Would you like to know what you were up to in your past lives? Are you curious about any agreements or sole contracts you may have entered into that you're unaware of in this present life? The next chapter has definitely been written for you.

Chapter 7: Timelines, Past Lives, and Soul Contracts

"Stop wasting time! Time is growing short for you to accomplish what you came to Earth to do!"
   - Dolores Cannon, The Three Waves of Volunteers, and the New Earth

What's the point of exploring alternate timelines? Why do your past lives matter? Do soul contracts hold any water if you don't even remember them? Are they still binding? There are many benefits to learning about timelines, your possible past lives, and soul contracts that you may be a part of. By examining your past lives and any parallel or alternate timelines, you understand yourself better. You think you know your full strength, but there's always more to be discovered. The more you know about these topics, the easier it will be to pick up on the patterns in your life and identify ways to grow beyond your limitations.

By examining your past lives and any parallel or alternate timelines, you understand yourself better.
https://pixabay.com/photos/time-clock-time-spiral-spiral-3103599/

Like it or not, your present challenges are connected to other lives that you have lived and are living right now. When you understand what happened in your past lives, you will find the logical explanation for those seemingly insurmountable obstacles you've had to contend with in this life and resolve them. Armed with this newfound knowledge, you'll be able to heal yourself of past traumas, which will allow you to finally experience growth in areas where you've been stagnant for too long.

Knowing your origins is a great way to discover your sense of purpose. You'll know where you came from and where you're heading. It will become easier to work out if you are living according to your soul's true purpose or not.

Finally, considering everyone has a history beyond what is known in this present incarnation, it's easier for you to extend compassion toward them. You realize they're the sum of all the characters they've played across lifetimes, just like who you are is the result of who you've been.

Do You Live Multiple Lives?

The first thing you must understand about existence is that time is an illusion. It may appear that you are living just one life, but you have more than one. According to Dolores Cannon, you are living many lives right now concurrently. Remember the idea of reincarnation? It is the spiritual concept that when you pass on, you return to Earth as a different person to learn new lessons or embody a new character.

If time is not linear and everything exists now, then that would suggest the idea of past lives is really the same as parallel lives. What people commonly refer to as "past lives" are parallel incarnations. So, as you read, note that both terms can be used interchangeably in this chapter.

What people commonly refer to as "past lives" are parallel incarnations.
https://pixabay.com/photos/body-ghost-soul-religion-woman-2976731/

You're just not aware of these other lives unless you peep in on yourself through past life regressions or dreams. Your consciousness is focused mostly here on your present incarnation on Earth, but that doesn't negate the existence of the other versions of you. Research Jane Roberts's work on the idea of the oversoul and its splinters so you can understand how this works.

As your body is made of multiple parts and organs, and each organ is made of multiple cells, you are one part out of an unfathomable number of lives, all connected to one soul. Put differently, if your oversoul is the ocean, your present awareness of this incarnation is one of the drops. You are one pinpoint of a grander, greater awareness than you currently have access to consciously. So, as you continue your spiritual evolution and your awareness expands, you begin to identify yourself in other individuals. The truth about your full self is that it is on God's plane where everything is united. There is no duality or separation. It is all one and the same consciousness.

How can you be certain that the idea of multiple timelines is a valid reality? The late Dolores Cannon did some amazing work in this field.

Working with hypnosis, she was able to help thousands of people with past life regressions. Throughout all these sessions, every participant gave her incredibly detailed narrations of their past lives across various cultures and epochs. Some of these people even spoke of past lives on other planets. The consistency of the results she got from her sessions indicates that there was no fabrication or fantasy involved. Why? Every story that was shared with Canon was later verified using historical research.

The people who worked with Dolores Cannon greatly benefited from the regression sessions. They found the connecting thread between what they experienced in their past or parallel lives and what they were facing in their present lives in terms of phobias, challenges, and gifts or talents that they inexplicably have. As these people revisited their past lives, they were able to resolve the trauma they experienced then. As a result, their present incarnation improved. They experienced profound healing and felt lighter and freer due to the emotional release from these sessions.

One interesting thing they all pointed out was their connection to the same set of souls across lifetimes, regardless of the setting or age. These souls changed roles from one lifetime to the next, switching from friends to family members and sometimes enemies. This raises the question, what is the point of these repeated dramas and reenactments of situations across reincarnations?

The whole point is the evolution of the soul. With each incarnation, whether you choose to call it a parallel life or a past life, you learn new important lessons that advance you to the next level of your spiritual development. As each person continues to develop towards their higher self, they contribute to the collective's growth.

Your soul is not bound by linear time. It experiences multiple realities simultaneously. It exists across multiple dimensions as well. When you die after playing your part in one incarnation, there is an in-between stage known as the *Life Review*. The stage is critical because it's where you go over the lessons that you have learned from the life you just left behind. It's where you experience your life through the eyes of everyone else with whom you've interacted with. You'll also get to connect with your loved ones from various lifetimes and plan what your next incarnation will be in this stage. The Life Review is not confined to the earthly concept of time.

Now you're probably wondering, how many reincarnations do you get? Dolores's work did not confirm any specific point at which you'll no longer have to incarnate. The reincarnation process does not end until your soul arrives at a point where it does not require physical experiences for its continuous expansion. When it gets to this point, it will not need to show up in this 3D universe. That doesn't mean the soul ceases to exist, but it goes on to other grander adventures that are beyond human comprehension. Your soul moves on to planes where it exists non-physically.

By Will or By Force? All about Soul Contracts

Your soul made the deliberate choice to incarnate on Earth. Some say you are only kept bound to Earth by beings known as archons, who are the ones who pretend to be your loved ones waiting for you at the light at the end of the tunnel when you pass on. They say these archons are here to trap you into the wheel of reincarnation so that you are forever condemned to this 3D experience, and you should never go into the light.

According to the work carried out by Dolores Cannon, it's clear that you deliberately decided to reincarnate here. This does not happen by chance, nor is it some punishment or trickery. Your soul is eternal, and its goal or desire is to know itself. There's no better way to know yourself than to try on many different roles and see who you are in those shoes. The desire to know yourself is natural because it stems from Unity, the Divine Source.

Remember, in the beginning, there was nothing and no one other than the creator, who or which was All-That-Is. The only way All-That-Is could know itself was to experience duality instead of its default unity. Therefore, it created All-That-It-Is-Not. Your soul is part of All-That-It-Is-Not, ultimately All-That-Is, and where you came from. Since Source desires to know itself through you, you, too, seek to know yourself, and you do this through your incarnations and steady evolution.

Now it's time to talk about soul contracts. Making the conscious decision to reemerge in a new incarnation means entering into a sole contract. It's not a piece of paper. It's symbolic of an agreement that you have between your soul, soul groups, and spirit guides. This contract clearly outlines everything you intend to learn from the journey or next incarnation. This symbolic agreement contains every significant experience you are meant to encounter and the patterns that will repeat themselves in the form of karma so that you can resolve them in this new incarnation.

There's no reason to be terrified at the concept of a soul contract because it is a road map that lets you know what opportunities you have to grow and become an even grander version of the person you are. The word "contract" makes it seem you don't have any choice but to follow that particular blueprint, but there is much room for flexibility and innovation.

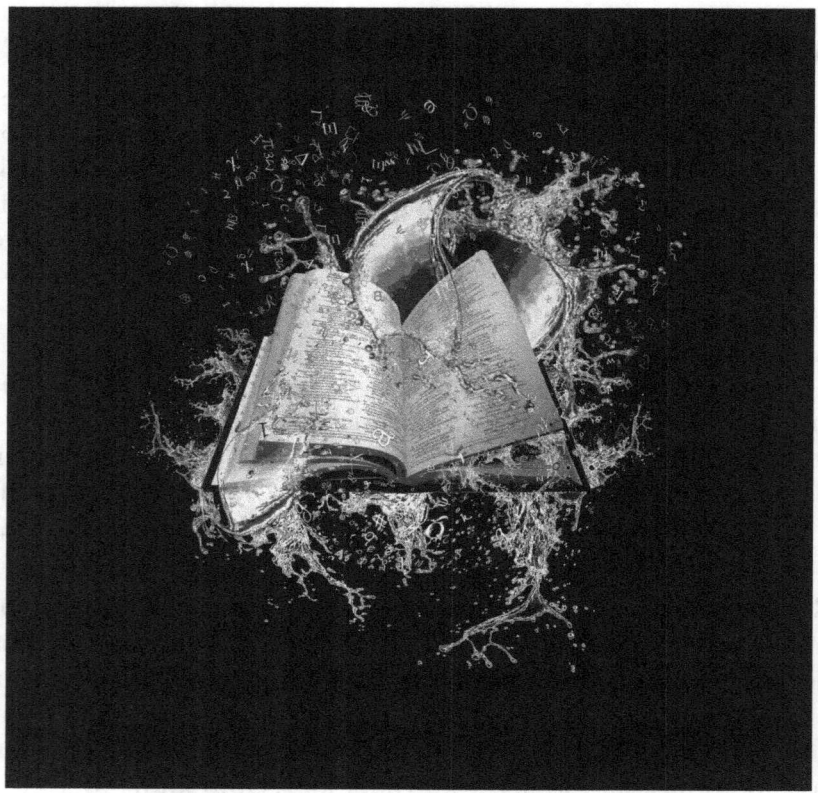

Per your soul contract, your soul chose to be on Earth.
https://pixabay.com/photos/bible-holy-spirit-jesus-hope-2989432/

Despite the existence of this agreement, you have free will. You get to decide what choices to make. You alone call the shots on how to navigate the challenges that present themselves to you. You decide whether to answer the call of divinity or ignore it. Clearly, you've chosen the former option because you are still reading this book. Every choice is critical to your soul's growth and will ultimately determine whether or not your contract will be fulfilled at the end of this incarnation.

A good question you may be asking yourself is why it's necessary to include challenges in this contract. Surely, there must be other ways to learn a lesson without difficulties and obstacles, right? You may find it beneficial to shift your attitude and perception of challenges. Every challenge and obstacle that you face in life is an opportunity for you to make decisions that help you grow. It's like going to the gym. The weights you lift are challenging, but you continue lifting them, and you become stronger with time. You'll be able to handle heavier things later on.

If you remember nothing else, realize your soul contract isn't set in stone. Depending on your experiences and the choices you must make, you could find extra lessons that were not part of the contract and may be inspired to renegotiate certain parts of that contract, working with your spirit guides and higher self who oversee the process. Remember, you are the observer. You always have free will, and the whole point of your existence is constant evolution from one incarnation to the next, even within individual incarnations.

Case Studies

The best way to appreciate past life regression is through learning from actual stories and case studies of people who have explored the memories from other incarnations. From their stories, you'll discover how past lives continue to impact present ones.

James Leininger: James's story is an interesting one centered on a series of nightmares that began plaguing him at the tender age of two. Night after night, he dreamed about being in an airplane crash and the final moments before losing his life.

With time, James shared more details about his nightmares with his parents. What he shared with them left them horrified. Their son was convinced that he had been a pilot in another life. Unfortunately, his craft was shot down while he was in flight.

The level of detail James recalled led his parents to conclude that he must have been describing a real experience. Among many other details, he told them the name of the aircraft he'd been flying, the carrier, and the full name of one of his friends who had been in the service with him.

After doing some research, they discovered many parallels between what James had shared with them and the life of another James from a different time – James M. Huston Jr. This was a pilot who had served in World War II and had passed away decades before the present James was born.

Two Hundred Children: The former head of the psychiatry department at the University of Virginia School of Medicine, Ian Stevenson, MD, had thoroughly documented about 200 cases of children who had birthmarks that matched up with wounds that the people they believed they were in their past lives had suffered.

Ian cross-referenced the birthmarks on these children with the medical records of the people who had passed away that the children claimed to have been in their past lives. One of the children was a boy who remembered that he'd suffered a headshot. To add credibility to the boy's story, there were birthmarks on the front and back of his head, the points of entry and exit for the bullet that brought about his demise. Ian also came across a woman who claimed to have been struck three times with an ax before she passed on. Guess what she had? There were three lines on her back.

As Ian continued his research, he noticed that a great number of the children who remembered past lives had inexplicable birthmarks that could not be explained by any infections, genetics, or any logical causes. His findings revealed that 35% of these children were suffering phobias that matched whatever the circumstances of their past life deaths were. For instance, if one child remembered being thrown from a great height, the odds were that they now have a phobia of heights.

Another fascinating thing he discovered was that many of these children seemed to have a preference for clothing or food from specific cultures, which they claim they used to be part of in their former lives. His work provides overwhelming evidence that past lives are real.

Jenny Cockell: Ever since Jenny was a little girl, she began to experience vivid details of one of the lives she had lived in her past, early in the 1900s. She recalled being an Irishwoman who went by the name Mary Sutton. Not only did Jenny remember her personal experiences as Mary, but she also recalled those of Mary's children, to whom she still felt deeply connected.

Jenny became intrigued enough to go on a journey to find the people she once thought of as family in her past life as Mary. After a lot of time and research, she eventually traced her identity to Ireland. She was able to meet up with these people, and they confirmed that her memories weren't fantastical; they were accurate, down to the last detail.

A Regression Technique to Connect with Your Past Life

So, you want to explore your past lives? Here's an excellent technique based on the work of Dolores Cannon. She came up with an interesting hypnosis method called the Quantum Healing Hypnosis Technique (QHHT), which is excellent for past-life regression, and the following technique is based on her work.

1. Get yourself into a relaxed meditative state using the meditation exercise you learned in an earlier chapter. You can sit or lie down. The choice is yours.
2. Once your body feels fully relaxed, imagine yourself in a peaceful place. Make it somewhere that resonates with you, whether a cabin in the woods, the beach, a forest, or wherever else. It should be somewhere you feel safe, secure, and calm.
3. From this safe place in your imagination, set your intention to explore whichever past life is most relevant to your present incarnation. You can call on your guides or higher self for assistance and tell them to show you what you need to see, which will be helpful for the evolution of your soul.
4. While in this space, allow your mind to travel. Don't try to control where your thoughts go. Allow feelings, impressions, and images to come to you freely. The scenes you see may show up in the space you have imagined, or you may be transported to a completely different place entirely. Don't have any expectations. Let things unfold however they will.
5. When you've finished, return your awareness to your physical body, take a few deep breaths to ground yourself, and then slowly open your eyes.
6. Write every thought in your journal as soon as possible to reflect on it later.

You now know how to check in on what's going on with your past or parallel lives. You understand the importance of doing this so that your present life can be more fulfilling and you can execute your soul contract flawlessly. So, what else is next? It's time to discover your higher purpose.

Chapter 8: Your Higher Purpose Revealed

"Focus not on what he or she does, but on keeping to your higher purpose. Your own purpose should seek harmony with nature itself. For this is the true road to freedom."

- Epictetus

Now that you have a clear grasp of your soul's journey through consciousness and infinity and are acquainted with your guides and higher self, it's time to discover your higher purpose. Is this something that continues to elude you? Do you feel confused about the point of your existence on this planet?

It's time to find the meaning behind your existence.
https://pixabay.com/photos/sky-love-spiritual-above-top-3983433/

You've worked out you are ultimately serving a goal of expansion, but the question is, what exactly are you supposed to be doing to make that happen? Where will you find the answer to that cosmic head-scratcher? This chapter will give you useful techniques to help you find a specific way you're meant to express your authentic self to live your purpose here on Earth.

Why You Should Look Within

Discovering the ultimate purpose of your soul isn't something straightforward. While there are several modalities you can use to arrive at the truth of your existence, it's not something as easy as following a step-by-step guide. It would be nice if it were as easy as following the instructions on a frozen dinner, popping it into the microwave, and letting it heat up until it's time to take it out.

Your soul's purpose is not found in a book or a movie. The reason it's not so cut and dried is that your soul has wisdom beyond words and logic. It doesn't care what your mind thinks it desires.

In searching for your soul's purpose, you could talk to as many gurus as you like, read all the books out there, and listen to endless hours of podcasts, yet all of that work could never trump inner work. Your soul's purpose is in you, meaning there's nowhere else to look but within.

The problem with relying on an external source of information is you will only achieve superficial alignment. You're artificially assigning yourself something to be passionate about. If you dig deep, you'll realize this "purpose" isn't resonating with your authentic self. You may start with verve and enthusiasm, but eventually, you'll notice a growing sense of dissatisfaction and emptiness in your heart.

Defining your source purpose should never be left to external forces. You came here with your unique blueprint for how you're supposed to live your life. You will lose your agency if you look outside of yourself for the answers you seek. This is the reason many complain of feeling lost.

When you allow the world outside of you or your circumstances to dictate what you do with your life, you will live a life with no meaning. You didn't come here to conform. You came here to transform – and you can only do that by being your authentic self.

As you begin seeking your soul's purpose, you should have a sense of reverence. You have to stay open, trusting that whatever is revealed to you is for your highest good. You need the right frame of mind. If you're serious about knowing why you're here, you must cultivate a state of mind that is calm and clear. This means it's time to put away distractions like your favorite social media app. You also have to stop doing other things you know are getting in the way of finding your why. You know what they are. Your soul's telling you right now.

A final point to be made before diving into the different modalities of soul-purpose exploration is that the process is a journey. It's not something that's set in stone. At certain times in your life, your soul's purpose will evolve, and it is your job to stay in tune with it and keep up with its evolution.

Soul Purpose Meditation

The world is full of stressed people. Stress is one of the reasons people find it difficult to discover their soul's purpose. Modern life is full of distractions and poor, subpar alternatives to spiritual gifts and exploration. There's probably a television in your home. How many times have you used it to numb yourself rather than listen to the part of you asking you to switch off and sit in silence?

If you give it some thought, you'll realize that humans have become androids. Why? Almost everyone has a cell phone, that little rectangle that might as well be called Distraction Central. Many are worried about artificial intelligence without realizing it has already been ruling their lives through that little device they carry.

On the surface, it may seem that access to digital information from a wide range of sources is a good thing. However, that can quickly lead to overwhelm. You pick up all kinds of ideas from all kinds of places, and the next thing you know, you're no longer yourself. You become a parrot, repeating other people's perspectives without giving it any thought of your own.

Even if you decide to put your phone away and go for a walk, billboards everywhere vie for your attention. There's so much noise in the world that it's difficult to hear your inner self. This is why meditation is one of the perfect routes to discovering your purpose.

Daily meditation helps you to reduce your stress levels, putting you in a frame of mind where it's easier to pick up on what your higher self is sharing. You shed all the opinions, ideas, and perspectives that aren't yours and are left with nothing but your *Self*.

Meditation is also helpful because it encourages you to self-reflect and improve your self-awareness. If you can't do that, you won't hear the intuitive nudges you receive from the Divine. With all that said, here's a meditation to help you reconnect with your soul's purpose and express your higher self. These instructions will help you discover your highest purpose.

1. Make sure you're not wearing anything uncomfortable or tight.
2. Find somewhere quiet, away from distractions and disturbances. Whether you sit or lie down during your meditation is up to you. Sit or lie down, but choose a position where you will stay awake.
3. Close your eyes and bring your attention to your breath. Breathe slowly and deeply. Inhale for four counts, hold for another four, and then exhale for four. Do you find the counts uncomfortable? In that case, inhale until your belly rises, hold your breath for as long as you can manage, and then exhale. You may notice your exhale is longer than your inhale. That's natural.
4. When you feel centered, picture yourself surrounded by a white light. This light feels warm to your skin. It fills your heart with sacred peace and joy. It is the light of your higher self.
5. Say in your mind or aloud, "Thank you for showing me my soul's purpose." As you repeat this like a mantra, contemplate what you're saying. By offering thanks, you're assuming and accepting that you've already received the answer you seek. So, this is how you learn your purpose – if not in this session, then in the coming days and weeks.
6. As you repeat this mantra, let the light envelope you and let it fill you on the inside as well.
7. Continue to bask in the feeling of gratitude until your meditation session is done. On some days, when you don't have enough time, a timer will be useful. On others, you may continue to bask in this feeling of thankfulness for as long as you like.
8. When you're ready, bring your attention back to your breath. Become more aware of your body. Give your fingers and toes a little wriggle to ground yourself. When you're ready, open your eyes.
9. Get your journal and write about your experience, including ideas and whatever visions or sensations you picked up.

Before moving on to the next method for discovering your soul's purpose, please understand that this is not usually something people discover in a day. That's not to say it's impossible to have that experience after your very first meditation session with this intention, but it's important to keep the right perspective and not pressure yourself with unrealistic expectations. Maintain an attitude of trust – divine nonchalance, if you will.

You've put forth the intention, and one thing about intentions is that they must be fulfilled. Each time the question of what you're supposed to do with your life arises in your mind, greet it with thanks in your heart. See the moments you feel confused about your purpose as the birthing pains of its revelation and choose to feel excited instead. This will quicken the manifestation of your answer.

Automatic Writing to Access Your Soul's Blueprint

Some call it automatic writing. Others call it psychography. Either way, it's the practice of reaching into yourself to draw out wisdom that is beyond your conscious awareness. It's connecting with your soul and your higher self to learn what is essential to know at this point in your life. Automatic writing is a beautiful way to figure out what you're supposed to be doing with your time on Earth. Whether you think this intelligence is coming from your soul, higher self, subconscious mind, or God, with automatic writing, you are allowing the intelligence of the Divine Source to flow through you.

There are so many reasons to take advantage of automatic writing.

1. It induces a state of calmness, grounding you in the present.
2. You'll experience uncommon clarity.
3. You're receiving guidance from the best sources through this practice.
4. Your third eye, throat, and heart chakras will open up and function even better as you practice.
5. You'll develop a more solid trust in your intuition and gut feelings.
6. You'll make wiser decisions than you used to.
7. Your psychic abilities will also improve.

As you practice automatic writing, you'll find it incredibly revealing. As a bonus, in the process of expressing messages from your higher consciousness, you'll be healed on so many levels. Many of the mental blocks, physical issues, and stagnancy people experience in life stem from refusing to express their inner selves. With automatic writing, you're allowing source energy to flow through you, and this energy automatically heals all wounds and opens all blocks.

How do you practice automatic writing? Specifically, how can you use this process to help you determine your soul's purpose? It's a straightforward process. Originally, this practice was done with a pen and paper, but with new technology, there's no reason you can't use a word-processing application. Some people prefer to do it the old way, with a good old-fashioned pen and paper, because something about the process of writing feels organic and helps them allow the messages to flow unhindered. It's up to you to practice and see what you prefer.

If you want to get the most out of automatic writing, you should forget about time. Don't expect that you must express everything you're supposed to learn in a matter of minutes. It's a process that will take as long as it takes. If you pressure yourself by trying to fit it all in a specific time frame, you will make it hard to pick up on what your higher self is telling you. Follow these steps to use automatic writing to discover your soul's grandest purpose.

1. Prepare the materials you'll be taking notes with. If you're taking notes with a digital device, please put it on airplane mode and set it to Do-Not-Disturb so you're not distracted by any notifications.
2. Bring your attention to your intention.
3. Take a few minutes to become centered by meditating. As with meditation, automatic writing requires an environment free from distractions and disturbances. So, if you need to inform other people you live with that you need a few moments alone, do so.
4. Now that you're grounded, pick up your writing materials.
5. From this calm state, write down your intention, which is to discover your highest purpose. If you prefer, you could phrase this as a question.
6. Keep writing your intention or question over and over while maintaining your centered state of mind and a soft focus on what you're doing. Alternatively, you could write the question just once and keep it in your mind. Wait for the messages to come.

7. At some point, you'll feel the urge to write something. Flow with that.
8. Throughout this process, your mind must be relaxed. There's no room for logic here, so don't feel like whatever's coming through onto the pages needs to make sense. Even if all you're getting are scribbles at first, trust that they will lead you to something profound with time.
9. At some point, you'll feel like there's nothing further to give. When this happens, don't be dismayed, and don't attempt to force the process to continue. Instead, offer thanks to your higher self and then review what you've written.

Discovering your purpose through psychography may require more than a few sessions, but it works effectively. Your expectations are everything. Don't interpret a seemingly fruitless session as a sign that this doesn't work. If you do, you might as well give up. Keeping your expectations positive and trusting that you already have your answer is a surefire way to get results. It's only a matter of time.

Finding Your Purpose Through Shamanic Journeying

There's no reason you can't discover the master plan for your life with shamanic journeying. After all, it's an excellent way to meet your guides and other wise and timeless beings who definitely know more about how life works and why you're here now as the personality you are.

If you choose to practice shamanic journeying to learn your soul's purpose, it's best to go to the Lower World. This world is associated with a deep level of transformation that results from introspection.

One of the main reasons many people aren't living up to their fullest potential or exploring their purpose is because of fear. They know they could be so much more, but they're held back by the implications of what it would mean to embody their full selves. This is why the Lower Realm is the best place to go. There, you can come face to face with your fears, discover what past traumatic events are holding you back, and heal from them.

Just as a seed must be planted in the earth before it shoots into the sky, so must you go into the womb of the Lower World first to find your why. You don't have to do this alone. You'll be accompanied by your guides. Here's how the process works.

1. You need to find a quiet place free from disturbances and distractions. If it helps, you can set the mood by dimming the lights, using candles, lighting incense, or whatever else will make you feel tuned in to the spiritual realm.
2. Play a shamanic drumming track in the background, or focus on the sound and feeling of your heartbeat.
3. Lie down or sit comfortably. Close your eyes and focus on taking deep, relaxing breaths, releasing tension with every exhale.
4. When you feel grounded in the moment, imagine a bubble of brilliant golden white light that surrounds you, keeping you safe and protected for the journey to come.
5. Bring your mind to your intention. Remember, the goal of this journey is to discover your soul's highest purpose. Firmly and softly state your intention.
6. In your mind's eye, see yourself at the base of the biggest tree you could possibly imagine. Notice the opening at the base of the tree. Walk towards it and enter through the opening.
7. Now you're inside the tree's trunk. Notice the stairs that lead down into the Lower Realm. Mindfully descend, feeling each step beneath your feet. Notice the sense of going deeper and deeper into the core of the universe.
8. As you journey down, you'll notice the world around you is changing. This tells you that you are approaching your destination.
9. You have now arrived. Take a moment to look around you and study what you see. Notice the environment as well as any sentient beings around, human or otherwise, and trust that you are safe and protected.
10. State your intention to meet your guides as you walk further into this realm from its entrance. When they show up, you'll know it because their energy will feel familiar and safe to you.
11. Once you meet your guides, ask them about your soul's purpose. Pay attention to how you feel and the thoughts that arise after asking. You don't always receive communication using words. Sometimes, it will be like a block of thought coming into your mind, and at other times, it will simply be a feeling or energy.

Whatever you receive, trust that it is your answer.

12. If the answer seems unclear, don't let that discourage you. Instead, thank your guides for offering you their time and guidance. Ask them to make the meaning of their message clearer to you over the coming days and weeks, and thank them for doing so. You should also thank them for their presence.
13. Return to the entrance of the Lower Realm and make your way back up the stairs. Once you're out of the World Tree, thank it for allowing you access to the Lower Realm.
14. Bring your attention back to your breath. Wiggle your toes and fingers to become more present in your body. When you're ready, open your eyes.
15. Get your journal and record every memory and feeling you received during your journey. Take a few moments to ponder the meaning of the message you got, putting it in the context of discovering your reason for being.

Note that you may not get the full picture of your guide's message to you after a session or two, but it is not something to worry about. Live every day with the intention of discovering and understanding their message more than before. Pay attention to the intuitive nudges and signs that come your way. This is how their answer will unfold and make itself plain to you.

Using Divination to Find Your Why

You've already learned a little bit about divination and how it works. It's an excellent way to find out why you are here. You could work with tarot readings, which require tarot cards. These cards include the Major and Minor Arcana, and each one has its own meaning.

Runes are another excellent choice, with each one representing a theme, word, and sound. Whether you choose tarot cards or runes, you could either interpret them individually or use groups of cards or runes to offer you context.

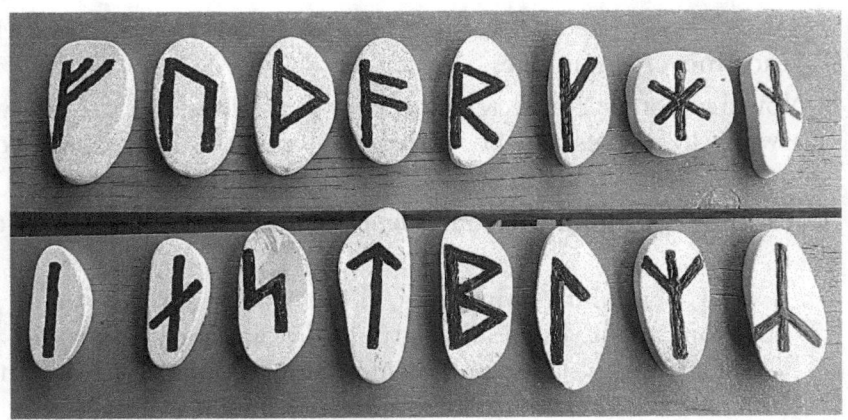

Runes can offer some context.

Runologe, CC BY-SA 4.0 <https://creativecommons.org/licenses/by-sa/4.0>, via Wikimedia Commons. https://commons.wikimedia.org/wiki/File:02_Runes_of_the_Younger_Futhark_painted_on_little_stones_-_Runen_des_j%C3%BCngeren_Futhark_auf_kleine_Steine_gemalt.jpg

One of the easiest and most accessible methods for these practices is pendulum reading. You'll need a pendulum, a weighted object that hangs at the end of a string. You could buy one or create a simple one at home using a piece of thread and a key with a hole. Pass the thread through the hole, then tie it securely with a knot. You now have a makeshift pendulum. No key? No problem. Any other heavy object you can hang from your thread will do. Here's how to use your pendulum:

1. Enter into a meditative state.
2. Take your pendulum in both hands – string and weight included.
3. Breathe golden white light onto the pendulum thrice, imagining that it clears it of all energies that will not serve you. This is how you consecrate it for your use alone and ensure you receive messages from your higher self and other guides who want good things for you.
4. Hold your pendulum in your dominant hand. Let the weight hang freely, swinging as it will.
5. Now, it's time to "calibrate" your pendulum. Ask it a question that could only be answered with a yes, like, "Is my name (your name here)?" Wait and observe the way that it moves.
6. Ask it a question that could only be answered with a no, like "Do I have two heads?" Now, observe the way it moves.

7. Ask two more sets of "yes" and "no" questions so you know what each movement implies.
8. Now that you've connected with your pendulum and know how it swings to say yes and no, set your intention to learn about your soul's purpose.
9. Ask your pendulum if your higher self and spiritual guides are present.
10. If your pendulum swings yes, begin asking simple yes or no questions about your soul's purpose. For instance, you could ask if you are meant to be in the entertainment industry. If it swings "no," keep asking about other industries until it swings "yes."

To make the most of this method, you may want to ask questions about the things you are naturally good at because the odds are they are part of your grand design and soul's plan.

5 Tips for Learning Why You're Here

You now have several tools you can use to discover your purpose. Regardless of what you choose, the following tips will help you to succeed.

1. **Pay Attention to the Things That Bring You Joy:** They're clues about what you're meant to be doing. Write about them in your journal when you discover them, and find ways to incorporate these activities into your everyday life and share them with others.
2. **Spend Time Meditating Every Day:** This practice is like sandpaper, polishing off all the unneeded roughness that keeps your purpose from shining brilliantly. It will help you see what matters and what doesn't. The answers you seek are within stillness, silence, and solitude.
3. **Get Creative:** You don't need to be the world's greatest artist, singer, writer, painter, or whatever else. Just find a way to tap into your creative side every day. Everyone has creative abilities within them. Express yourself through art, and you'll find clues about what matters to your soul.
4. Spend Time in a Natural Environment. Nature is a powerful gift. The more time you spend in a natural environment, the easier it will be to pick up on your soul's desires and plans. Your higher

self is always speaking to you. Whether you choose to be up in the mountains, by the seashore, or in the heart of the forest, you'll notice nature sharpens your inner ears to hear the guidance you carry within you.

5. **Keep an Open Mind:** If you've always preferred routine, it's time to shake things up. If you always say no to the new and unfamiliar, it's time to ask yourself why. Could it be that your ego knows that's where your true purpose lies? Start saying yes to new opportunities and experiences and see what exciting paths they lead you down.

Chapter 9: Daily Rituals for Conscious Living

At the start of this book, you learned about consciousness, exploring different perspectives and descriptions. You've learned that consciousness is awareness and that you can be aware of being one thing or another. You also discovered the connection between consciousness and quantum physics, finding the threads that connect these subjects. You also learned about quantum brain mechanics, which explains the origins of consciousness.

You discovered the state of superposition, which is when a particle exists in every possible state it could all at once, only choosing one state in response to an observer and their expectations through the wave function collapse. You understand how entanglement works, but what are the implications? If you're observing something and expecting it to present in a certain way, it does, and then every other thing quantumly entangled with it must mirror that one thing.

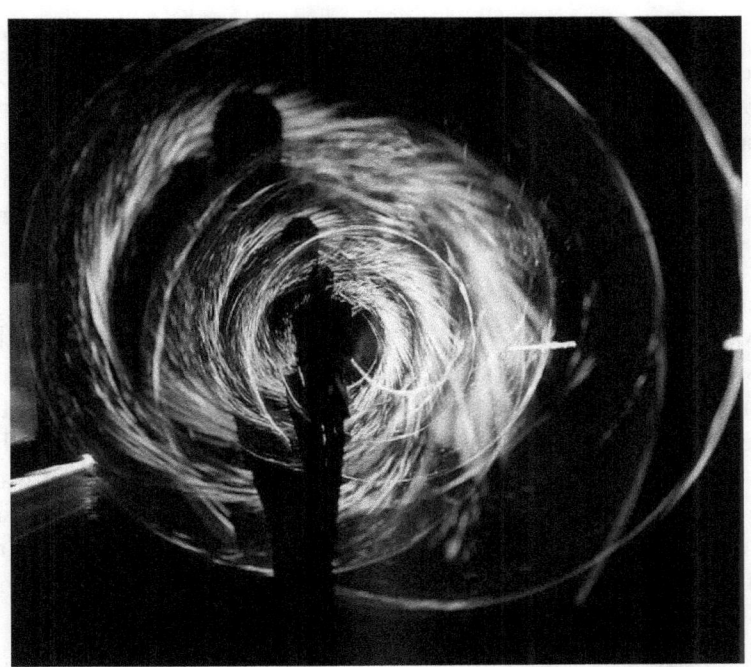

Tapping into the infinite intelligence of higher consciousness will lead you to live a life that gives you joy and fulfillment.

https://www.pexels.com/photo/silhouette-of-person-holding-sparkler-digital-wallpaepr-266429/

To make things plain, every possible version of you and your life exists at the same time. If you've been conscious of being a poor, starving artist, you've used the observer effect to cause a wave collapse function where you live only as a poor, starving artist as opposed to anything else. With entanglement always in action, everything in your life mirrors your identity as an artist who cannot afford to make ends meet.

The implication is that if you want to be a successful artist, you have to "observe" yourself as that. You have to become "conscious" of vision by tapping into higher consciousness, the field of infinite possibility, selecting this preferred state of being, and then causing the wave function collapse that changes your world to reflect your new state of abundance.

You also learned about higher consciousness, and hopefully, you've realized there's no reason to condemn yourself to the struggles of living a life purely from your ego's limited perspective and assumptions of what's possible for you. These practices help you become aware of your higher self, break through limiting paradigms, tap into the infinite intelligence of higher consciousness, and live a life that gives you joy and fulfillment.

To see powerful, permanent change, you need a daily ritual incorporating these powerful quantum physics and consciousness concepts. This chapter will help you with suggestions for practices to make a non-negotiable part of your day. By creating a consistent ritual for your spiritual evolution, there's no limit to the heights you can attain, and you'll turn everything you once considered "impossible" into reality.

Morning Rituals

Start every day with a ritual and observe how your life changes with time. It's easier to practice your preferred spiritual exercises first thing in the morning before you do anything else because the energy you put out at the start of your day will pave the way for good experiences. At the very least, it will help you handle any negativity better. Suppose you wait until you're in the middle of your day to practice. In that case, you'll have difficulty getting the most out of your ritual – and that's a double guarantee if you've already gone through situations that put you in a bad mood.

If you kick start your day with a spiritual practice, you automatically put yourself in a state of heightened awareness and are more conscious of your choices throughout the day. You're also less susceptible to letting negative emotions get the better of you if some undesirable situation triggers them. You already know about meditation. What else could you do first thing in the morning?

Set Positive Intentions: Your intention is how you want something to play out. It's how you'd prefer to experience your day. Even if you're feeling a little doubtful about the power of all this, you could at least set an intention for one thing that you know is within your control, which is your emotional state. By starting your day with the intention to embody a specific emotion or state of being, you give yourself a better chance of feeling how you want to feel.

As you set positive intentions for your emotional state, pay attention to how your day goes. Journaling is an excellent practice that will help you. At the end of each day, reflect on the intention you started with and review how you handled yourself. The more you practice setting positive intentions, the more you'll notice your feelings line up with whatever you intended. This result should give you more than enough evidence of the power of setting positive intentions. From this point on, you can practice setting intentions for specific situations you'd like to experience.

How do you set a positive intention? When you wake up in the morning, immediately begin meditating. Once you feel grounded and your mind is still, turn your attention to your intention. If it helps, you can summarize it in a single word. Then, repeat this word while contemplating what it means to you until you begin to feel it.

Notice where this feeling comes from in your body. Then, move the feeling around your body from head to toe. Imagine it like a white light. After moving this light around, you allow it to permeate your entire body. You can end this session by offering thanks. If you're still battling with the idea of entities other than humans, at least trust that through quantum entanglement, your day should line up with your intention.

You can also set intentions at the end of your day for a good night's rest, dreams, communicating with your guides through visions or dreams, astral travel, etc. You can set intentions whenever you want to. The more you practice and see results, the more likely it is that you'll get used to setting intentions on the fly at different points of your day. You could set them up for productive meetings, interesting interactions, an enjoyable lunch, etc.

Gratitude: Gratitude is the cheat code to manifest whatever your heart desires easily and quickly. Many people assume you should only be thankful after receiving something, but did you know you can reverse-engineer the process? Think of it like this. Your desire is a particle. Your thankfulness for having received the desire is another particle. Both particles are quantumly entangled. By choosing to be thankful for receiving your desire, even if you don't have physical evidence of it yet, you are causing a wave function collapse that will lead to the manifestation of the desire.

For people who struggle with all kinds of manifestation techniques, gratitude is a simple shortcut. So, what do you desire? Whether it's for your day to go a particular way or for something more specific and tangible, try gratitude. A simple way to practice this is to first get into your centered state from meditation and then say, "Thank you," while contemplating what it is you're thankful for.

One of the reasons gratitude is so effective is because you're skipping the middle bits of how your desire will come to be and cutting to the aftermath when you've already received it. So, make this a daily practice.

Another way to practice gratitude is by making lists of things for which you are thankful. It doesn't have to be a long list. Even just listing three to five things every day that you appreciate will go a long way to activating the magic of gratitude in your life. How? You'll experience even more to be grateful for. There may be days when you feel like you can't come up with a single thing to appreciate. There's no reason to beat yourself up for that! It's enough to revisit old lists you've made and let your heart be full of thanks for them.

A common mistake people make is assuming that it's about the words. Without actually feeling thankful, you could say "thank you" until the cows come home and not experience any of the lovely gifts gratitude gives you. So, how do you generate the feeling? Recognizing all the reasons why you're thankful is a good thing, and how – despite many people not having those same blessings – you get to experience them!

Mind-Body Connection Practices

Many people experience anxiety, fear, and worry because they are in their heads and not in their bodies. Mind-body connection practices are designed to move you from that chaotic mental space into just being in the here and now, the same way your body is.

Yoga: Yoga will show you in real-time how your mind and body are connected. As you practice it each day, you'll discover that you're not only getting fitter but also more present and grounded. Remember, this state of presence is essential for remaining connected to higher consciousness, which is why you picked up this book in the first place. Visit your local Yoga instructors. Try a class with several of them to find the best fit for you.

Yoga will show you in real-time how your mind and body are connected.
https://www.pexels.com/photo/woman-practicing-yoga-3822906/

Tai Chi: Tai Chi is a moving meditation that heals your body. This Chinese martial art puts you firmly in your body, giving your mind a chance to go to bed. As a result, you'll take the relaxation you feel from each session into other aspects of your life, operating with a calm and clear mind – the kind of mind that's conducive to picking up on messages from the spirit world. The inner peace a consistent Tai Chi practice offers you is beyond compare. Every move is synchronized to the breath, making it impossible to be anything but present. Look out for classes around you to find one where you feel comfortable.

Breathwork: Breathwork is another stress-relieving practice that will help you maintain your higher consciousness connection. It's one way to practice mindfulness, requiring you to control your breath in various ways. If you're like most people, you probably take shallow breaths. The problem with breathing this way is that you activate your autonomic nervous system, which means you are constantly stressed out. You keep your body stuck in the fight-flight-freeze-fawn state. These responses are great when you're in danger, but when you're stuck in this state for too long, it's terrible for your health.

Breathwork: will help you activate your parasympathetic nervous system, which allows you to rest and feel at ease. What's more, it puts you in a meditative state, keeping you in the present where it's easier to release negative emotions, beliefs, thoughts, and behaviors that keep you from living authentically. Here are a few versions of breathwork practices you can take advantage of right away.

1. **Diaphragmatic Breathing:** Lie flat on your back, with a hand on your chest and the other on your stomach while you breathe. To inhale, go slowly and use your nostrils. You should feel your stomach lifting your hand. To exhale, release the breath slowly through your slightly open mouth so the hand on your belly goes back down. Keep going for as long as you want.

2. **4-4-4-4- Breathing:** While lying flat on your back, inhale through your nostrils for four counts, hold your breath for four counts, exhale through your slightly open mouth for four counts, and hold your breath for four counts. Repeat this process, stopping when you're ready to or when your timer goes off.

Law of Attraction Visualization Techniques

Visualization involves using your imagination to see the version of the world you'd prefer to be in. When you visualize something, you are using the observer effect to select your reality through the wave function collapse mechanism. You're channeling your formless consciousness (I AM) toward embodying a specific form (that). This is the esoteric interpretation of the Biblical phrase, "I Am that I Am."

Visualization involves using your imagination to see the version of the world you'd prefer to be in.
designed by freepik. https://www.freepik.com/free-photo/collage-numerology-concept_35858713.htm#

You can use vision boards to visualize. Clip every picture and article that sums up the essence of what you want to create and put them up where you can see it first thing in the morning and last thing at night.

Another method is the "State Akin to Sleep" technique by Neville Goddard. It's a simple, three-step process:

1. Know what you want.
2. Construct a scene that could only happen after you receive what you want (not before and not during). Make it a concise scene. If you want a promotion, the scene could be your boss shaking your hand and saying, "Congratulations."
3. Lie down and convince yourself that you're sleepy by repeating, "I feel sleepy." Then, from this drowsy state, loop the scene you

created over and over, making sure you pay attention to the sights, sounds, and other sensations in that scene.

Other Rituals

1. Try taking midday awareness breaks. In the middle of your day, you could meditate, visualize, set intentions, or do anything else to help you realign with higher consciousness.

2. Afternoon and evening reflections are great for developing self-awareness. You could talk to your higher self through channeling, using a recording app to play back those conversations later or transcribe them automatically. With this practice, you're reflecting on the events of the day so far and reminding yourself of your intention to remain aware of your interconnection with others, your guides, your higher self, and, of course, higher consciousness.

3. Dreamwork is a great tool to incorporate as a ritual. Begin by writing down whatever you remember of your dreams every night to improve your recall. If you think you don't dream, at least write down how you feel when you wake up. When you begin recalling your dreams, you can set the intention to use this state to do your higher consciousness work every night before bed or whenever you want to take a nap.

With these daily rituals, you'll experience an increase in your consciousness and self-awareness. You go from living a life full of "accidents" to living on purpose and in alignment with your highest ideals. Consistency is the secret to getting results with these rituals, and the more you practice, the more pieces of the puzzle to your ultimate purpose you'll collect and put together.

Conclusion

You've been given every tool possible to begin the process of living consciously. The fact that you've read up to this point suggests that you will likely experience the spiritual expansion you desire.

There may be days when you don't feel like you're in the mood to practice your rituals. This is a natural part of being human. Remember, connecting to higher consciousness is more of an ebb and flow. There's no reason to beat yourself up for feeling like you've fallen off the wagon. On the days when you find it difficult to follow through, if you can commit at least three to five minutes to one practice, that should still keep you progressing – but that's no excuse to become complacent either.

This book is only a guideline and not a rule book. So, if you feel intuitively led to tweak certain practices or try something new, follow your hunch. Remember, no one can lead you better than your higher self. Trust every intuitive nudge you receive. Learn to do this without question, and you'll be amazed at the magical world that reveals itself to you.

There are so many resources available to help you along your journey. An open mind and avail yourself of everyone you come across. Whether you're reading a book or watching a video, always check in with your gut. How will your soul let you know what messages to keep and what to discard? Follow what is designed for you rather than do everything recommended to you because you're hoping something sticks. Even in this book, certain exercises may have caught your interest more than others. Your interest is a clue from your higher self, telling you that you should explore this.

You're about to begin a journey that will pay dividends. Ask anyone who's found their connection to higher consciousness, and they will tell you they have no idea how they could have lived without it.

If you're struggling with anything, whether it's consistency or focus, don't forget you're not alone. You have guides to assist you toward the fulfillment of your grand design. You could never be too much trouble to them. Ask, and it will be given – every time. Thank yourself for having the courage to begin this adventure. It's nothing to sneeze at, but in the end, you'll be glad you answered the call of the source of all life.

Here's another book by Mari Silva that you might like

Your Free Gift
(only available for a limited time)

Thanks for getting this book! If you want to learn more about various spirituality topics, then join Mari Silva's community and get a free guided meditation MP3 for awakening your third eye. This guided meditation mp3 is designed to open and strengthen ones third eye so you can experience a higher state of consciousness. Simply visit the link below the image to get started.

https://spiritualityspot.com/meditation

Or, Scan the QR code!

References

Acacio, J., Montemayor, C., & Springerlink (Online Service. (2019). Quanta and Mind: Essays on the Connection between Quantum Mechanics and Consciousness. Springer International Publishing.

Bertoldi, C. (2012). Inside the Other Side: Soul Contracts, Life Lessons, and How Dead People Help Us, Between Here and Heaven. Harper Collins.

Byrne, L. (2011). Angels in My Hair: A Memoir. Three Rivers Press.

Cannon, D. (1993). Between Death & Life: Conversations with a Spirit. Ozark Mountain Publishing.

Cannon, D. (2009). Five Lives Remembered. Ozark Mountain Publishing.

Carrington, H., & Muldoon, S. J. (1981). The Phenomena of Astral Projection. Sun Publishing (NM).

Crabbé, R. (2019). The Three Shamanic Worlds. RoelCrabbe.com. https://www.roelcrabbe.com/the-three-shamanic-worlds/

Delamothe, M. (2023). Shamanic Journeying and Astral Projection: What's the Difference? SignsMystery. https://signsmystery.com/shamanic-astral-difference/

Gergar, L. (2010). What is the Higher Self? Channel Higher Self. https://channelhigherself.com/blog/what-is-the-higher-self-2/

Gizzi, C. (2016). What Is Higher Consciousness and How Can We Access It? Fearless Soul – Inspirational Music & Life-Changing Thoughts. https://iamfearlesssoul.com/what-is-higher-consciousness-and-how-can-we-access-it/

Greene, B. (2012). The Hidden Reality: Parallel Universes and the Deep Laws of the Cosmos. Penguin, Impr. , Cop.

Gribbin, J. R. (2009). In Search of the Multiverse: Parallel Worlds, Hidden Dimensions, and the Ultimate Quest for the Frontiers of Reality. Wiley.

Ingerman, S. (2020). Shamanic Journeying: A Beginner's Guide. Sounds True.

Itzhak Bentov. (2000). A Brief Tour of Higher Consciousness: A Cosmic Book on the Mechanics of Creation. Inner Traditions.

Luna, A. (2017). Automatic Writing: How to Channel Your Soul's Wisdom. LonerWolf. https://lonerwolf.com/automatic-writing/

Luna, A. (2021). Soul Purpose: 5 Gateways to Finding Your Destiny. LonerWolf. https://lonerwolf.com/soul-purpose/

Psychic Radar. (2023). Exploring Past Life Regression: Unveiling the Secrets of Previous Lifetimes. Psychic Radar. https://psychicradar.com/articles/exploring-past-life-regression/

Roberts, J. (1994). Seth Speaks: The Eternal Validity of the Soul. Amber-Allen Publ., New World Library.

Rochelle, K. (2023). Understanding Spirit Guides. Positively Kimberly. https://www.positivelykimberly.com/understanding-spirit-guides/#How_to_Connect_with_Your_Spirit_Guides

Scalisi, A. (2022, July 15). Complete List of 22 Abraham Hicks Processes + How To Use Them. The Haven Shoppe. https://thehavenshoppe.com/22-abraham-hicks-processes/

Sharma, S. (2023). Breathwork 101: 5 Simple Breathwork Techniques for Beginners. Calm Sage – Your Guide to Mental and Emotional Well-Being. https://www.calmsage.com/breathwork-techniques/

Thomas, J. J. (2022). Higher Consciousness Demystified. Heart Speak. https://medium.com/heart-speak/higher-consciousness-demystified-80042c9fc9be#bypass

Tolle, E. (2016). A New Earth: Awakening to Your Life's Purpose. London, UK Penguin Books.

Tolle, E. (2018). The Power of Now: A Guide to Spiritual Enlightenment. Hachette Australia

www.ingramcontent.com/pod-product-compliance
Lightning Source LLC
Chambersburg PA
CBHW072152200426
43209CB00052B/1152